OUT OF THE BLUE

THE ESSENCE AND AMBITION OF FINNISH DESIGN

gestalten

OUT OF THE BLUE

THE ESSENCE AND AMBITION OF FINNISH DESIGN

GRAPHIC DESIGN, CONCEPT AND RESEARCH
Nokia Design Team:
Paramdeep Bahia
Hugh Miller
Lisbet Tonner
Bradley Zimber

EDITOR
Laura Houseley

COMMISSIONING EDITOR
Marko Ahtisaari

SUB EDITOR
Christian Smith

CONTRIBUTING WRITER
Dan Hill

NOKIA PROJECT MANAGEMENT
Robert Ellis
Alexandra Tyrer

SPECIAL THANKS
Aapo Bovellan
Anthony Dalby
Chris Merrick
Tiina Ruohonen
Stephen White

CONSULTANCY
Gestalten:
Robert Klanten
Sven Ehmann
Ferdi van Heerden

COVER DESIGN
Gestalten:
Robert Klanten

PRINTING
Offsetdruckerei Grammlich, Pliezhausen
Made in Germany

PAPER
120 g/m² Munken Polar
130 g/m² LuxoSatin (cover)

PUBLISHED BY
Gestalten, Berlin 2014

ISBN
978-3-89955-457-1

© 2014 Nokia. All rights reserved.

© Die Gestalten Verlag GmbH & Co. KG, Berlin 2014

All rights reserved. No part of this publication may be reproduced or transmitted in any form or by any means, electronic or mechanical, including photocopy or any storage and retrieval system, without permission in writing from the publisher.

Respect copyrights, encourage creativity!

For more information, please visit www.gestalten.com.

Bibliographic information published by the Deutsche Nationalbibliothek. The Deutsche Nationalbibliothek lists this publication in the Deutsche Nationalbibliografie; detailed bibliographic data are available online at www.dnb.d-nb.de.

This book was printed on paper certified by the FSC®.

Gestalten is a climate-neutral company. We collaborate with the non-profit carbon offset provider myclimate (www.myclimate.org) to neutralise the company's carbon footprint produced through our worldwide business activities by investing in projects that reduce CO_2 emissions (www.gestalten.com/myclimate).

INTRODUCTION

FOREWORD BY MARKO AHTISAARI
25–27

FINLAND DEBRIEF
28–29

DESIGNING FINNISHNESS BY DAN HILL
31–45

SKILLS AND TRADITIONS

OIVA TOIKA
48–59

KARI VIRTANEN
60–69

NATHALIE LAHDENMÄKI
70–73

THE KALEVALA
74–83

KLAUS HAAPANIEMI
84–93

FUJIWO ISHIMOTO
94–101

RUT BRYK
102–105

PUUKKO
106–111

SIMO HEIKKILÄ
112–117

DESIGNER AND INDUSTRY

HARRI KOSKINEN
120–129

EERO AARNIO
130–141

MARIMEKKO
142–165

MARIMEKKO INVENTORY
166–173

YRJÖ KUKKAPURO
174–183

VUOKKO NURMESNIEMI
184–193

ARTEK
194–215

NOKIA
216–247

COMMUNITY AND PLACE

SAUNA
250–259

TALKOOT
260–265

ANTTO MELASNIEMI
266–279

PAAVO LEHTONEN
280–285

TURNTABLE URBAN GARDEN
286–291

AVANTO ARCHITECTS
292–299

SAUNALAHTI SCHOOL
300–303

DEMOCRATIC DESIGN

KAJ FRANCK
306–315

TAPIO WIRKKALA
316–321

ALVAR AALTO
322–333

ILMARI TAPIOVAARA
334–339

ARABIA AND IITTALA
340–353

THE EPIC AND THE BOLD

SANNA ANNUKKA
356–363

YOUNG FINNISH DESIGNERS
364–381

WOODISM
382–383

SAMUJI
384–391

IVANA HELSINKI
392–397

**FOREWORD
MARKO AHTISAARI
HEAD OF NOKIA DESIGN
2009–2013**

Nokia made this book to better understand ourselves. By exploring the culture of Finnish design we felt we could learn a little more about our own ways of seeing, our own culture. What is it that we see that others do not? And how does that result in the products that we make?

Out Of The Blue is an original, intimate look at what makes Finnish design Finnish. It is neither comprehensive nor encyclopedic, but rather our personal take on the design and culture that surrounds us.

Nokia, as a company, has always been a product of Finland. The character, culture and nature of this place have shaped our business and continue to influence us: Whether it is Finland's lack of a proper monarchic tradition and he hierarchy and ornamentation that come with that; whether it is the almost primitive purity of approach or the peace and quiet we seek in nature as a people who only recently moved into cities; or whether it is Tapio Wirkkala's essential, material-led creations, Kaj Franck's peerless craft or Alvar Aalto's focus on the gentle structure of the everyday.

The Nokia Design Studio has evolved and been defined over many years by the assured guidance of Frank Nuovo and Alastair Curtis before me and by the talented individuals we have each had the pleasure to lead. Nokia Design has crafted and continues to craft some of the most distinctive and meaningful products in the world.

In the studio we strive to make products in which the digital and the physical form a harmonious whole. These are products that are pure and human, yet advanced, and built better in every way. They are products for emotional communication, products that connect people. These values have clear roots in the traditions of Finnish design.

To understand Finnish design, past and present, is to understand a wider cultural identity. The chapters of Out Of The Blue look at the skills, traditions and ambitions that are the origins of contemporary Finnish design and the work of both well-known and emerging talents that encapsulate its enduring values. Dan Hill's thoughtful essay further explores the cultural context that is so important to Finnish design.

When we began work on this book, we could barely imagine that Nokia's mobile device business would soon be sold to Microsoft. What began as a casual project exploring the origins of our design approach has ended as something even more vital: a documentation of Nokia's Finnish heredity during a historic period of change for the company and for the European technology industry itself.

We are not nostalgic. The Finnish design world we are part of is vibrant and fast moving, and the following pages illustrate that. The lessons taught by iconic creative thinkers from our past are still relevant and continue to shape the future. The values and aspiration of Finnish design are perhaps more relevant than ever before.

But Finnish design cannot afford to be complacent. As Vuokko Nurmesniemi recently said, with a glint in her eye, 'no one has really figured out these electric things yet!' Nicely put. If it is to remain culturally relevant, design needs to embrace the world of connected, interactive things: to push forward with fundamental research in materials, cognition, connectivity and power, and to produce more social, emotive and natural modes of interacting with connected objects. Finnish design, engineering and human sciences are well placed to invent this future.

Recently, on a walk by the seaside in Helsinki's Siltasaari with designer Harri Koskinen, I expressed my wish that talented Finnish designers, him included, should work more on software and interaction; that the world would be better for it. Harri was quick to reply: 'And you, my friend, should work more on furniture and objects.' We stopped and laughed.

Standing by the sea's edge, watching the water mirror our work, we do see things more clearly. Out of the blue. Great things will follow.

Read about the culture of design in the Nokia Design Studios on page 216.

FINLAND DEBRIEF

Local short form
Suomi/Finland

Population
5.4 million

Language
Finnish (official) 91%
Swedish (official) 5.4%
Sami is the mother tongue of 1,700 indigenous Sami people.

CAPITAL CITY

Helsinki (population 1.25 million in the metropolitan area.)

Independence
6 December 1917 (previously a grand duchy in the Russian Empire).

Government
Republic, parliamentary democracy.

KEY FEATURES

High standard of education, social security and healthcare all financed by the state.

Currency
The only Nordic EU member to use the euro.

Education
There is only one mandatory standardised test in Finland, taken at the age of 16.

Industry
Technology industries are the most important industrial sector in Finland, with 290,000 people directly employed in the sector.

Landmass and water
338,000 sq km
188,000 lakes
180,000 islands

LAND COVERAGE

According to 2009 figures, just 2% of Finland is built upon. In comparison, The Netherlands has 13% of its landmass covered in buildings, Germany 7% and Spain 4%.

North
Situated between the 60th and 70th parallels of latitude, Finland is one of the nothern-most countries on the European continent.

Wooden architecture
The Kerimäki Church in Finland is the world's largest wooden church.

Climate
In winter, the coldest days can be between -45°C and -50°C in Lapland. In summer, temperature highs are between 32°C and 35°C in the Finnish interior.

Midnight sun and polar nights
The midnight sun is a natural phenomenon occurring north of the Arctic Circle and south of the Antarctic Circle. And, around the time of the summer solstice, if the weather is fair, the sun is visible for a full 24 hours. The opposite phenomenon, the polar night, occurs in winter when the sun stays below the horizon all day.

SAUNA

2.2 million saunas (one for every 2.5 people).

Forest
Forests cover 75% of the country. This makes Finland the most heavily forested country in Europe, with 20 million hectares of productive forest.

Trees
Dominant trees are the Scots pine, the Norway spruce and birch.

Ecology
Finland recycles 90% of all recyclable bottles and cans.

Connected
There are around 9.7 million mobile phone subscriptions in Finland, more than two for every person.

NO PUBLIC PHONES

In 2007, the last public phones were removed from Finland's streets. The discontinuation was credited to the widespread ownership of mobile phones. Most of the kiosks were recycled, although a small number of them were converted into saunas, garden bars and even rain shelters for outdoor shooting ranges.

Internet
Since 2010, every Finn has had the right to access a 1Mbps broadband connection. Finland has vowed to connect everyone to a 100Mbps connection by 2015. Accessing the internet has become a 'fundamental right' for all people in Finland.

GAMES

Angry Birds by Rovio is a Finnish invention and was a low-budget concept, costing just over €100,000 to be developed and completed.

Acquired Taste
Suomen Salmiakkiyhdistys (The Finnish Salty Liquorice Association) is the only organisation of its kind and is a non-profit consumer organisation, founded in 1997.

CAFFEINE

Finland is the biggest consumer of coffee and the only country that has made coffee breaks at work statutory. The average Finn drinks four to five cups of coffee per day.

Competition
Finland holds world championships for wife carrying, mobile phone throwing, mosquito catching, swamp soccer, boot throwing, air guitar and, until recently, sauna.

TANGO

The tango is very popular in Finland. There are approximately 2,000 tango clubs in Finland and the Seinäjoki Tangomarkkinat is one of the largest tango festivals anywhere. The five-day event attracts over 100,000 tango-mad visitors each year.

News
'Nuntii Latini', or the news in Latin, is a weekly review of world news on Finnish national radio read in classical Latin, the only broadcast of its kind in the world.

Music
Hevisaurus is a heavy metal band for the under tens. The band dress as dinosaurs and play to youngsters between two and nine years old.

Suffrage
Finland was the first European country to grant women the right of suffrage and the first to allow women to be electoral candidates.

FAILURE DAY

Each year on 13 October Finns celebrate Failure Day. 'We must envision a new culture where people not only embrace and openly discuss failures, but also reward bravery despite failure and actively share lessons', says the manifesto.

*All facts correct at time of publication

Dan Hill is a designer and urbanist. He has held leadership positions at Fabrica, Sitra (the Finnish Innovation Fund), Arup, Monocle and the BBC. At Sitra, he was part of the influential Strategic Design Unit from 2011–2012, exploring how design might enable positive systemic change, via projects such as Low2No, Brickstarter, Design Exchange, and Open Kitchen. He has written many books, essays and articles on the intersections between design, cities, media and technology, and produces the blog 'City of Sound'. For Out Of The Blue, Hill reflects on Finnishness, both real and perceived, and the junction where design and a national identity meet.

DESIGNING FINNISHNESS BY DAN HILL

THE ESSENTIAL

'Finland is what remains of something else: take away the Slavs, the Scandinavians, the Orthodox, the Catholics, the sea salt, the birch forests, scrape away a few hundred thousand tonnes of granite and what you are left with is Finland.'[1]
– Diego Marani

1. New Finnish Grammar by Diego Marani, Dedalus Europe 2011.

The elements feature so strongly in Finland that elemental is all it is at times.

The essence of Finnishness sometimes appears to be essence itself, to be about the essential, as if wrought from the granite and gneiss that make up its huge landmass. Hard, opaque, taciturn, stubborn, resilient: it is a naturally unforgiving environment, beautiful in its own way, but hardly blessed. In 'This is Finland', one of the popular Finnish children's books featuring the maniacal characters Tatu and Patu, our heroes 'bake Finland' in a Finland-shaped baking tray full of bedrock, clay, peat, moraine, pine, spruce and birch, with lakes poured on top. The elements feature so strongly in Finland that elemental is all it is at times.

When dealing with the essential, necessity does not breed frippery, skittishness or carelessness. It breeds purpose, momentum, independence and a belief in technical strength; the art of know-how, nous, savoir-faire. Building on the pragmatic foundations required to survive, the formalisation of this techne via the technocratic, engineered, managerial framework of modernity leads to the production of Finland—and Finnishness. Rem Koolhaas said recently that 'national identity has seemingly been sacrificed to modernity'. Finland is one of the few countries whose national identity is a form of modernity. Finland was born alongside the beginnings of design itself (design in the contemporary sense). Its timing was impeccable in terms of a national culture being expressed in industrially designed (rather than crafted) objects. Hence the potency of Marimekko, Iittala, Kone, Fiskars, Artek, Nokia. Both Finland and modernism were formally born and developed concurrently after the First World War.

We admire fortitude in the face of such harsh environmental conditions and the ability to create global commercial empires and world-leading education systems in a country of 'only' 5.5 million people, located at the chilly peripheries of traditional power structures. Fortitude is emerging with strength from centuries spent under the thumb of empires to the west and to the east, having urbanised late with a culture attuned to living apart in wilderness rather than together in cities.

We in some way elide the story of Finnishness with the clichéd national personality traits of sisu, silence, solitude or insobriety, as I just have.

SECOND AND THIRD GLANCES

But for each cliché there is a counterpoint, and Finnishness possesses a far richer and far more fluid set of dynamics. Yet these cannot be detected, at first glance.

Indeed, it is not immediately obvious why Helsinki is increasingly seen as such a good city by global taste-makers.[2] Save for a few gems, its architecture is not particularly appealing: the buildings are often massive, hulking mega-structures covering entire blocks. On top of that, the shops shut early and the food is highly variable. It certainly isn't the weather.

2. Helsinki topped Monocle's 2011 Quality of Life survey, which rated it the world's 'most liveable city'. The Economist Intelligence Unit rated it at number seven in its Global Liveability Ranking in 2011. And it was appointed World Design Capital in 2012.

Helsinki is a city of second glances. It is a city that must be worked at. Its delights can be found in unlikely courtyards hidden behind dog-leg entrances; in cosy cafés and nurseries secreted behind nondescript, even foreboding, entrances; in patterns of geometric brick motifs and expressive typography tucked under oxidised copper awnings above your head; at vibrant, pop-up events in what would otherwise be an empty park or disused kioski. Its grandeur is not in the typical urban set pieces of rivers, harbours or grand squares, but instead in the small, everyday details that reveal themselves slowly.

When you look again, the first realisation is that Finnishness is entirely designed.

Imagine you were asked to design a city from scratch. Perhaps you might start with the small things—say, the door handles of Helsinki, which Juhani Pallasmaa describes as the handshake of the building—and work your way up from there. Creating a city that looks after the small, quiet and mundane things would mean starting with people in mind—which is why we make cities in the first place, after all. It is at this discreet level that Helsinki begins to come alive—at the second and third glances—and that holds for Finnishness in general.

Finnishness is a culture that rewards and resides in the oblique, the buried, the peripheral. To some extent, it must be unpeeled like the layers of an onion. Its beauty is to be found in hidden juxtapositions, like the pearl, grit and briny water within the rough exterior of the oyster.

When you look again, the first realisation is that Finnishness is entirely designed, an creation that substitutes for a much deeper, far more varied slew of cultures across the country and the region. Architect Martti Kalliala writes of the 'kansallinen projekti',[3] essentially a continual process of designing Finland that started around 1917: '[T]he idea of Finland becomes the vessel for fabricating a new cultural and linguistic identity. Led by a handful of artists, writers, poets, composers, architects and journalists, the group puts its skills to use: an immaterial country built of

3. National project.

4. Solution 239–246: Finland: The Welfare Game by Martti Kalliala with Jenna Sutela and Tuomas Toivonen, Sternberg Press 2011.

language, voice and image… nation-crafting through creative work leads to virgin territory: write the first play, paint the first national landscapes; compose the first symphony, hymn, anthem; publish the first newspaper, etc… The cultural project transforms into a political one.'[4]

Finnishness is a confection of real folk tales and folk tales invented for the purpose of creating a particular folk. Yet almost all nation states are designed. Flags, anthems, borders, laws, songs, events and governments all are prototypes at some point and only become a form of reality with time. But if we understand Finnishness as a design, it means it might be redesigned. Moreover, design itself is also an important key component— albeit a particularly twentieth century kind of design.

If Finnishness was rapidly prototyped a century ago, what were the qualities that resulted from this combination of active nation-crafting and existing essential conditions? We might find a few core characteristics that are both true and untrue. And in the spirit of the third glance, what if each provided a clue as to where Finnishness might evolve next? Not as a prediction, and certainly not as a direction, but as a possible future, drawing insight from the shift in twenty-first century design away from simple objects, products and services and towards contexts, conditions, interactions and frameworks. What questions should we ask of Finnishness now? For perhaps design is really about framing the right questions as much as anything else.

While we can say Finnishness was in a sense designed along with Finland, it is also, at the same time, much older than Finland.

FROM HARD TO SOFT

The Finnish language is significantly older. And, of course, the one thing that non-Finns know about the Finnish language is that it is impenetrable, legendarily obscure, emblematic of an apparent hardness or flintiness.

5. A kind of vodka made from barley that is now Finland's most popular spirit. Homemade Koskenkorva was commonplace during Finland's prohibition era, from 1919 to 1932.

Perhaps as a result of that, Diego Marani's idiosyncratic novel New Finnish Grammar gives us the best contemporary insight into Finnishness. In Marani's book, Finnishness is articulated for the reader by a frequently drunk pastor who filters every aspect of his culture through the prism of the Finnish language, as well as through copious amounts of Koskenkorva.[5] While Finnishness may be invented, he states that the language itself was not.

6. Marani 2011, ibid.

'[O]ther languages are merely a temporary scaffolding for meaning. Not so for Finnish: Finnish was not invented. The sounds of our language were around us, in nature, in the woods, in the pull of the sea, in the call of the wild, in the sound of the falling snow. All we did was to bring them together and bend them to our needs.'[6]

At its core are a group of ancient words: small, soft words describing the body, the landscape, the weather, the world: kuu (moon/month), suu (mouth), puu (tree), sää (weather), jää (ice), pää (head), kivi (stone), mäki (hill), joki (river), lahti (bay), järvi (lake), saari (island).

Hard conditions begat a hard language and a facility with hard materials.

This emphasis on the physical, the body, objects within a landscape, and their various conditions, is an interesting starting point for a culture. Is this why Finnishness also focuses on objects and their material qualities, the body and the landscape? In what Marani describes as 'chipped sounds, words eaten away by ice and silence' we might find the origins of a later facility with objects, with architecture and, in particular, with a purist form of both, a design oriented around authenticity and the qualities of natural materials. Equally, the emphasis on the body would generate the form of humanist modernism associated with brands like Artek, which aimed to 'support and nourish human beings' physical and psychological well-being… blending functionalism with form and sculptural simplicity with the emotional warmth of wood.'

Hard conditions begat a hard language and a facility with hard materials. Yet those soft words also begat softness, through a comfort with the body and the ephemeral conditions of weather, flora and fauna.

Hardness also applies to the environmental conditions Finland is subjected to. It is, of course, insanely cold. Yet everything is built to withstand it, from clothing and transport to urban planning and buildings. I have been colder in Australian and Italian houses than I ever was in our Helsinki apartment. Equally, the delights of the Finnish summer, which can be perfectly warm, if a little brief, means it is entirely possible to witness a 60-degree centigrade temperature swing across the year.

Thanks to engineering, that swing in conditions is not a problem. Conquering such conditions means that engineering itself has an exalted status within Finnishness.

Yet the next challenge is beyond engineering, beyond dealing with the hardness and difficulty of Finnish conditions. It deals with soft systems, social systems. 'The idea of Helsinki is radical: a new capital for a new nation; an ideal city built from a tabula rasa; an orthogonal grid laid over the topographic granite of an irregular peninsula; a window to the West and the East; a showcase and platform for a political, social, cultural and architectural experiment on a grand scale.'[7]

7. Kalliala 2011, ibid.

Tsar Alexander I had designated, and in effect created, Helsinki as a kind of special political zone, just as Shenzhen would be a special economic zone for China almost two centuries later. He designed it to be an autonomous grand duchy, a merging of Russian order and liberal European values picked up during his schooling in Switzerland. It was a prototype for politics.

While hard boundaries changed in largely obvious ways, the soft system of politics draped over what would become the Republic of Finland suggested a design of decision-making itself.

> The 'Finnish silence' is an essential component of Finnishness, perhaps derived from the solitude that marks much of the Finns' existence.

Scroll forward many decades to recent years and a practice of 'strategic design'—the design of decision-making cultures—would emerge in Finland, partly courtesy of Sitra, the Finnish Innovation Fund. The concern here is not with the production of objects, services, buildings and cities, but with the conditions that would enable those things to address new kinds of highly complex and interdependent problems. Part of a growing international movement often looking at the design of the public sector, it feels like a different form of design, focused not only on those 'hard' outcomes, but also on the soft systems of culture, management, services and the organisation that enables them. It is a clear departure from the obvious tangibility of what people recognise as Finnish design.

Is it possible to connect the institutions that have nurtured Finnish design to the nation's history of designing cultures, which is barely recognised as design at all? How to train a generation capable of articulating the architecture of 'wicked problems',[8] and not simply the architecture of buildings?

8. Dilemmas in a General Theory of Planning, Horst Rittel and Melvin Webber 1973.

This is the first step in evolving Finnishness—dealing with soft systems as well as hard outcomes.

FROM SILENT TO SOCIAL

That those Finnish words are 'eaten away by silence' is also important. The 'Finnish silence' is an essential component of Finnishness, perhaps derived from the solitude that marks much of the Finns' existence. The giant landmass, the small population and the late urbanisation all conspire to create an everyday life that, only a few generations ago, was based on not seeing many other people at all for days on end.

Daniel Dennett suggests that 'talking, and not talking, is what makes us human'. Dennett means 'not talking' in order to conceal or obscure deliberately. But in Finnishness it is often simply... not talking. Foreigners are often thrown by a Finn's ability to deploy a gaping silence in the middle of a conversation—like the old theatre joke when the narrator utters 'night falls' followed by a sudden drop of the curtain. This comfort with silence is appealing in the context of cultures that revel in small talk instead, filling each moment with something, anything—essentially with the chaff of shallowness. At the same time, it can reinforce the idea that Finnishness is socially awkward. Though it should be noted that this taciturn characteristic of Finnish communication is most frequently associated with the males of the species.

Juhani Pallasmaa, who has perhaps written more influentially than any other Finnish architect, recalls of his childhood that 'Tapio Wirkkala, the legendary designer, was an elder brother for me, and he taught me the importance of craft. As I had spent the decisive years of my childhood at my farmer grandfather's humble farm, I shared a love of nature, solitude and silence with Tapio.'[9]

9. Fragments: Collage and Discontinuity in Architectural Imagery by Juhani Pallasmaa, edited by Matteo Zambelli, Giavedone Editori 2012.

This is just about the most Finnish paragraph one could imagine: Craft, nature, solitude, silence.

Yet at second or third glance, Finnishness is noisy. The roar of rally cars in a forest; ice hockey fans stumbling around raucously in a freezing fountain after any win over Sweden; the thunderous volume of Finland's numerous variants on death metal, pagan metal, doom metal; Pan Sonic playing a gig from an armoured car on a 5000-watt sound system. In terms of contemporary music, at least, Finland is primarily associated with the especially loud.

From the most prevalent cultural export of recent years, the soundscape of Angry Birds is anything but silent. The unhinged genius of its orchestral score leaps maniacally around, sometimes merged with franchise space-operatic themes, whereas in-game a frenzied backdrop of crazed grunts, snarls, yelps, battle cries and screams provides no respite at all.

No, Finnishness need not even be quiet, never mind silent.

Objects are no longer silent either. As Kazys Varnelis says, 'technology is our modernity now' and, for Finnishness, defined around a previous form of modernity, this is a step change, beyond engineering and into an understanding of objects that have emotional expressiveness and responsiveness, variable character and identity. Objects and spaces will soon be social, just as people are. The solid melting into air.

FROM FLAT TO FLEXIBLE

With Finnishness, sociality is generally rather humbler and quieter, a more delicate skein of connection which is strong, yet not obvious. The calmness of the päiväkoti (or nursery) on a dark afternoon, the hiss and sigh of the sauna, the coffee shop that sounds more like a library than its chattering and clattering Italian counterpart. This low intensity hum of connection is then punctuated raucously through a shameless inability to drink alcohol properly, seen most clearly in the wild partying of the Vappu (first of May) celebrations.

That existing pattern—low-intensity connectivity to the point of barely being there, with occasional explosions—might need a broader range in order to work with social objects. The Finnish silence is an intriguing, and not obvious, starting point for thinking about objects no longer being silent—yet that is where the opportunity is.

Finns are relatively new to urbanisation—traditionally, the idealised association with nature, purity, silence and darkness means a rejection of cities and urbanism, perhaps betrayed when Alvar Aalto talked of 'the inhuman dandy-purism of the big cities'—so Finnishness has yet to develop a broader social range and a greater 'natural' comfort with urbanisation, a richer variety of urban living. There is plenty of evidence—the extraordinary Ravintolapäivä pop-up restaurant day, for example—of weak signals in this direction. Would this more diverse, more richly social sense of Finnishness enable a unique facility with social object-making?

> The structure of society is flat, with relatively high levels of income equality and mobility within a non-stratified culture.

With a few exceptions, Finland's terrain is flat as a berry-strewn pancake, an enormous landmass patterned mainly with forest, lake and mosquito-rich swamps, with little in the way of mountains. The vocal patterns within Finnish, despite the extravagant rolling 'r's and the propensity for sudden robust singing, are largely flat. The Baltic, at the coastline anyway, is not exactly a sea marked by rollers and breakers. City skylines, save for the odd spire, are also a carefully regulated flat envelope, around six storeys tall. Architectural quality is also very even. In general, save for a few gems, buildings are rarely great, but also rarely bad. The structure of society is flat, with relatively high levels of income equality and mobility within a non-stratified culture. This latter is often described as the Nordic model, from whose wellsprings a pleasing flatness emerges, a so-called 'spirit-level' culture. Yet that flatness can also work against a richer sense of Finnishness. Innovation is difficult in a culture so attuned to everyone getting the same experience. This may or may not be a problem, but it is a fact. And it manifests itself in some odd ways. For instance, in the city.

Innovation is difficult in a culture so attuned to everyone getting the same experience.

Finnish city planning culture remains in a dark age of postwar planning. It builds efficiently and effectively, but largely without pleasure, without diversity and without adventure. Finland can build sustainable buildings as well as anybody—at least as sustainable buildings are usually framed, which is largely unsustainable, of course—but its towns and cities are largely full of stolidly 'efficient' glass and steel boxes, punctured only by the occasional jewel such as the Temppeliaukio Church and Finlandia Hall in Helsinki, the Rovaniemi City Library or the Sibelius Hall in Lahti. There's a suffocating flatness to the imagination of most of those who control the making of the city, reinforced by homogeneity among those designers who get to design and build it. The number of foreign firms or designers who might enrich the country's architectural DNA is generally far too low (only a couple of significant Finnish buildings have been designed by non-Finns), just as the insularity and politics of some public and private sector cultures have meant a look inwards rather than outwards. In Helsinki, which was essentially created and reinforced as an emblem of the broader national project and so works as a kind of sign and signifier of Finnishness, the population has been relatively homogeneously Finnish for most of its existence.

Yet in recent years, Helsinki's population has begun to diversify rapidly. And this is a good thing, as encouraging diversity may be a key strategy for developing a resilient culture, generating a richer decision-making platform, as well as flushing out the very essence of the city itself. Richard Sennett describes how Aristotle thought of the city as a synoikismos, a coming together of people from diverse family tribes, each oikos having its own history, allegiances, property. For Aristotle, the definition of a city is a place 'composed of different kinds of men; similar people cannot bring a city into existence.' Likewise, an economic diversity is beginning to emerge via a concerted push towards developing a 'startup culture' alongside numerous social innovation ventures.

So just as the ongoing success of Helsinki will be predicated on how it genuinely absorbs diversity while retaining a sense of provenance, given that Helsinki is a form of prototyping ground and testbed for what Finnishness can be, we might speculate that challenging flatness will be central to Finland's ongoing success too. How to enable the spikes of innovation that might design tomorrow's better public services as Finnishness evolves? How to create a culture of openness to new ideas, to entrepreneurs, side bets, the unknown and ambiguity rather than certainty? And how to absorb the best of this into a new strain of Finnishness?

FROM PURE TO ROUGH

Finnishness, with its emphasis on humbleness, simplicity, authenticity, natural processes and materials, is oriented towards an idea of purity.

At first glance, even Finnish objects themselves seem to be about a purity of form and colour. Kaj Franck's classic crockery set Teema is essentially defined by pure colour, with the form pared back to its essential ur-possibility. The ur-cup. The ur-bowl. By backgrounding formal expression, it foregrounds its use, its context, its part in a social ritual.

Pallasmaa thought the same of homes: 'The experience of a home is structured by distinct activities—cooking, eating, socialising, reading, storing, sleeping, intimate acts—not by visual elements.'[10] The home's purity of form and colour is a red herring, instead enabling a rich variety of activities.

10. The Eyes of the Skin: Architecture and the Senses by Juhani Pallasmaa, John Wiley & Sons 2005.

Yet a form of purity, albeit somewhat warped, is also behind the populist politics of the Finns. It speaks of a desire for authenticity, which may be in part due to its relatively short existence as a national culture, and in part due to the belief that Finnishness is unique and fundamentally close to nature. As Timo Salli, designer and professor at Aalto University, says of his fellow countrymen: 'We're isolated, we have a strange language and we still have one foot in the forest.'

The latter appears extremely strong at first glance. An afternoon spent on the islands can feel entirely remote. In winter it feels like endless white snow, with the boundary of land and sea blurred by ice, patterned with scrawny sketches of black trees as depth markers and topped with perfect blue sky. Summer feels fecund in response. Juhani Pallasmaa notes: 'The forest condition, the rich spaces, forms, sounds and smells of the forest are a kind of a mental massage and therapy for me.'

The darkness that pervades Finland describes an almost primal, pure relationship with nature, related to the forest.

The archetypal Finnish dwelling—the summer cottage, or mökki—exemplifies this purity through nature. A condition of the mökki is that it must be difficult to get there and that you are hidden once you do. It should never be obvious on the shoreline; only its small satellite, a lake- or sea-side sauna, might betray its existence. It should be shrouded in trees, perhaps glimpsed only at night in fleeting flickers of light through dense thickets of pine. Then there is the purity of the darkness.

'But he could no longer forget the one terrible thing—that the sun didn't rise any longer. Yes, it's true; morning after morning broke in a kind of grey twilight and melted back again into the long, winter night—but the sun never showed himself. He was lost, simply lost; perhaps he had rolled out into space. At first Moomintroll refused to believe it. He waited a long time.'[11]

11. Moominland Midwinter by Tove Jansson 1957.

The darkness that pervades Finland describes an almost primal, pure relationship with nature, related to the forest. The notion of the dark forest was reinforced by 'discovered' national epic The Kalevala, and further through Jean Sibelius's readings of its core characters such as Tapio, the forest spirit, in his tone poem Tapiola, which he described in a quatrain thus: 'Widespread they stand, the Northland's dusky forests, Ancient, mysterious, brooding savage dreams; Within them dwells the Forest's mighty God, And wood-sprites in the gloom weave magic secrets.'

With half the year spent in that velvety gloom and dusk, even if no longer in the forest for most Finns, the darkness is an utterly defining characteristic. Pallasmaa suggests some connection between darkness and community, noting how 'the dark womb' of some buildings may create a 'mystical and mythological sense of community… a sense of solidarity.'[12]

12. Pallasmaa 2005, ibid.

As a European, or other Westerner, there are many occasions in Finland when you feel that you are clearly in the East, or at least the extremity of the West. And so it is not that unlikely to find shared fondness for darkness, as well as steam, solitude and silence, in Finnish and Eastern bathing cultures. Junichiro Tanizaki describes the perfect and purposeful gloom of the traditional Japanese toilet thus: 'Surrounded by tranquil walls and finely grained wood, one looks out on to blue skies and green leaves… a degree of dimness, absolute cleanliness, and quiet so complete one can hear the hum of a mosquito.'[13]

13. In Praise of Shadows by Junichiro Tanizaki 1933.

Purity of nature, of experience and physical purity all convene when described by Leonard Koren in Undesigning the Bath: 'In the Finnish sauna, for example, 'rules' are passed down from father to son about the proper sauna atmosphere (the quiet inside; maintain the sauna as you would a pure and holy place), the essential purpose of the sauna (purification of body and soul), and so on.'[14] Tanizaki also notes how the beauty of a Japanese room is not immediately perceptible, at first glance, to Westerners: 'It betrays a failure to comprehend the mystery of shadows.' At second and third glance, the darkness of Japanese rooms, and perhaps the darkness of Finnishness, reveal a different, arguably deeper form of beauty.

14. Undesigning the Bath by Leonard Koren, Stone Bridge Press 1996.

Of course, the corollary of its position on Earth is also the endless sunlight of summer. Again, each note of Finnishness has, if not its opposite, its 'adjacent possibility'. These coveted elemental conditions are all part of the myth of Finnish purity and deep harmony with nature.

And myth it is, as Finland must also deal with the paradox that it possesses one of the highest carbon footprints per capita in Europe. And near that 'pure' mökki, the Baltic Sea is in a state of near collapse, as polluted as anywhere. While Finns may blame this on industry and agricultural run-off elsewhere, their industry and agriculture is also complicit in this.

On a more positive note, to counter all the purported quiet, austere purity of much Finnish modernism, there is also the explosion of colour in Marimekko, and the wit and warmth of Eero Aarnio's and Oiva Toikka's work.

> There is a genuine wildness and weirdness at the core of Finnishness, which sets it apart from other Nordic cultures that are essentially far 'safer'.

Moreover, there is a genuine wildness and weirdness at the core of Finnishness, which sets it apart from other Nordic cultures that are essentially far 'safer'. It's not simply the ancient bear-worshipping, forest-dwelling pagan traditions that comprise the footnotes for The Kalevala, but also the gothic Hel Yes! food-meets-pagan cabaret shows; shock rock band Lordi winning the Eurovision song contest; an expertise in anything involving a helmet; Paavoharju's forest disco; SantaPark built in what seems like a vast nuclear bunker under Rovaniemi; the game mechanics and environment that underpins Angry Birds; the unlikely fondness for tango. Most of these images are well known and sometimes a little over-played. Yet they are also all true.

So that purity is often delightfully offset by roughness, eccentricity and the unpredictable. Given the occasional ambiguity of daily existence in Finland, despite the striving for clarity and purity, might the culture develop an equal and explicit comfort in inefficiency as well as efficiency, in the unplanned as well as the planned?

KNOWING WHAT TO DO WHEN THERE IS NOTHING TO DO

'The press conference is over, and in comes Jari Litmanen, from behind the door. And I looked at his face and I looked at his eyes, and I recognised something in those eyes. And I thought, this is a man with a great will-power. Because he was not shy, not timid, but he was modest. He is not a man who will raise his voice, or bang with his fist on the table and say, 'We do it this way'. No, he was more of a diplomat, not wanting to be a leader, but being a leader.'[15] – David Endt, former AFC Ajax manager

15. David Endt, Former AFC Ajax manager, on legendary Finnish footballer Jari Litmanen in an interview with YLE TV2, 2010.

Finland has proven that it can take care of itself locally and globally.

Finland has proven that it can take care of itself locally and globally. At home, its sheer existence, never mind the extent to which it has lately thrived, is a tribute to fortitude, guile and determination. Globally, through Nokia, Kone, Rovio and others, through its diplomatic and political leadership, and through its design scene in general, it has punched well above its weight. Having been a reluctant leader, like Litmanen, will Finland once again step up to help define a new age, a post-industrial or re-industrial age? Unlike in 1917, there are few obvious external drivers to force Finns to define Finnishness. So where will the desire for change come from?

Finland, and Finnishness, is not immune to the problems facing other European countries: the Eurocrisis, domestic xenophobia, industrial strife. Challenging these is difficult for an engineering culture not yet used to working with uncertainty, or in collaboration.

That requires a sense of openness to ambiguity, to non-planning, which is quite unlike the traditional mode of Finnishness. And yet there are also valuable cues in Finnishness, such as in the design—or undesign, as Leonard Koren would have it—of Finnish sauna culture: 'Making nature really means letting nature happen, since nature, the ultimate master of interactive complexity, is organised along principles too inscrutable for us to make from scratch… Extraordinary baths… are created by natural geologic processes or by composers of sensory stimulation working in an intuitive, poetic, open-minded—undesign—manner.'[16]

16. Koren, ibid.

Equally, the päiväkoti day-care system[17] demonstrates a learning environment built with an agile structure that can follow where children wish to lead. The role of expertise—and every teacher in Finnish education is a highly qualified expert—is not to control or enforce a national curriculum, but to react, shape, nurture and inspire. As such, it could be a blueprint not only for education generally, but also for developing a culture comfortable with divergent learning, with exploration and experiment, with a broader social and emotional range, and with ambiguity.

17. A state-run system available for all children under the age of seven in Finland.

Chess grandmaster Savielly Tartakower once said: 'Tactics is knowing what to do when there is something to do, strategy is knowing what to do when there is nothing to do.' Indeed, Finland's early development was driven by tactics; survival, consolidation and then growth in the face of a clear set of 'things to do': defeat the conditions, resist the neighbours, rebuild after war.

With that came success, comfort and then perhaps the inevitable lack of drive. The country is relatively well off and stable, and perhaps a little complacent given the recent accolades.

> With its strong technical research sector, and expertise in both materials and software, Finland is well placed.

Design in recent years has seen a shift towards the ephemeral and social: interaction design, service design, user-experience design, strategic design and so on. Conversely, there has been a return to the physical, albeit altered and transformed by that new modernity, with that possibility of newly hybrid 'things': digital/physical hybrids possessing a familiar materiality yet allied with responsiveness, awareness and character by virtue of having the internet embedded within. With its strong technical research sector, and expertise in both materials and software, Finland is well placed. Connect the power of its nascent nanotech research sector—interestingly, derived from its expertise with wood—to a richer Finnish design culture capable of sketching social objects, social services and social spaces, and its potential becomes tangible, just as with the 1930s modernism that fused the science and engineering of the day with design in order to produce Artek.

Finnish design could be stretched to encompass these new directions, the aforementioned reversals towards openness, ambiguity, sociality, flexibility and softness. Given that unique DNA of Finnishness—both designed and undesigned, both old and young—Finland is at an interesting juncture. The next phase, then, is knowing what to do despite the appearance of not having anything to do.

Buckminster Fuller, a guest at Sitra's first design-led event at Helsinki's Suomenlinna island fortress in 1968, once said: 'The best way to predict the future is to design it.' Finland has done this once before. And now might be exactly the right time to do it again.

The word 'designer' is a relatively recent addition to the Finnish vocabulary. Previously, the master cabinet-makers, ryijy rug-makers and glass-blowers were anonymous authors—but no less creative and influential for that. Contemporary designers—among them Kari Virtanen, who says 'the valuable craftsmanship of a cabinet-maker serves as my starting point'—demonstrate how present this craft past is.

Finland's craft heritage is as old as it is rich. And vital. This nation of 'farmers' has always taken pride in self-sufficiency and many Finns remember how, just a generation or two ago, their grandfathers built their own homes and made their own furniture and tools. The value of utility in design today stems from the original purpose of these crafts.

Finland's successful design industries have evolved from traditional craft production in wood, glass and textiles. And much is being done today to keep craft skills alive, from Simo Heikkilä's consideration of the Sami knife to Klaus Haapaniemi's reappropriation of folk imagery.

SKILLS AND TRADITION

Oiva Toikka has proclaimed that he is 'lazy'. But the vast retrospective of his work that filled Helsinki's Design Museum to the rafters a few years ago suggests otherwise. His work has taken many forms. Originally trained in ceramics, he has also been a prolific stage and costume designer. But he is best known for his glasswork, particularly and most recently for his much-loved Iittala Birds.

Toikka is surely the designer that most Finns could name and whose work they are most likely to own—or covet. He has become something of a legend, not only because of the enduring appeal of his work, but also for the spirit in which he created it, combining greatness with humility and warmth.

MASTER OF MANY
OIVA TOIKKA

What happened at the beginning of your career that led you to work with glass?
Originally I wanted to paint, but that was only a dream. Next I wanted to be a graphic designer; then I chose the ceramics department of the art school. I was there for one year before I had to go into the army. When I came back, I asked if I could go to the graphics department instead. The school said yes, but my teacher said no.

Were you happy there?
Yes, very. I was there for three years. I met my wife there and I had wonderful colleagues. Then my teacher pressed me to go to work for Arabia. The top designers in ceramics were there at the time.

Kaj Franck, for example?
It was the beginning of the 1950s. Kaj Franck was there, but he was specialising in utility then. Rut Bryk was excellent. I was so curious and I visited people there very often. I was visiting a lot. Some got tired of me and said that I visited too much. But, anyway, I was there 12 months and I really liked it. But there was one thing that was wrong: I was too lazy. I didn't work hard enough to get commissions. And our family was finding it hard to survive. So I went to become a teacher in Lapland. Then there was an advertisement in the newspaper for the Nuutajärvi glass factory. I'm a country boy, so I had no difficulties with being in the country. My wife was also pretty pleased.

Had you done any work in glass before that?
No. There was no department for glass at the school.

What type of glass did you work on originally?
Utility pieces. Pieces like Flora and Fauna. They succeeded in the market: they sold well. And they sell well now.

Was function the most important element of those early designs?
Yes. That was why they were made with pressed glass.

Did what Kaj Frank was doing have any affect on you?
Yes, in a way. We talked a lot about things. But I always had the feeling that I never learnt anything. I didn't copy him, but he influenced me.

In his way of thinking?
He was very clear. I have met very few people who can see utility in all materials like he did: in enamel, glass, ceramic, wood, everything.

When did you begin to produce art pieces at Nuutajärvi?
Kaj Franck had made art pieces all the time. Then I began to do so too and we had an exhibition together. All the other artists also made unique pieces there.

When did you begin to make the birds?
It was about 1971. I didn't really have any idea that this was going to be such a big success. But people love animals. Anyway, it has been a wonderful time. The people around this project have been excellent.

Is there a special relationship between you and the blowers?
Yes. We trust each other. And there is understanding too.

Who is your favourite glass-blower? Can you say?
The glass-blower I'm working with at the moment.

How do you work with him? How does the process work?
My way is that I don't make drawings. I go there and we talk and talk. I say, let's begin with that. He makes one and then we begin to change it. So it becomes a new item.

No sketches, no drawing, just talking?
Drawings are not necessary at all. The blower doesn't want that either. But we talk a lot. I love that way of working.

Do the most beautiful things happen when they're unplanned?
Yes. Mistakes can be very healthy. It is important that the pieces are practical. If they are not beautiful, they work anyway and you learn. Like you learn to love a person who is not beautiful and suddenly you realise, oh, what a wonderful person. There are many designers who say that perfection is their big theme. For me it has never been so.

With the materials that you work in, it would be very difficult to achieve perfection. You wouldn't choose glass.
I don't know what perfection is. That's the problem.

Have you ever blown?
No. When I first went to the Nuutajärvi factory, I thought that I might have to blow. But I was so shy that I didn't begin and then I started having a problem with my back and that meant I never learnt. I'm pleased because they do it much better. I have always had good luck with the people I work with. Of course, at the theatre I also had an excellent partner too: Lisbeth Landefort.

You have designed the costumes for the National Opera?
Costumes and graphics.

Of all that you've done, do you have a favourite type of work?
No. My favourite is whatever I happen to be working on at the moment. I get inspiration from the people I work with. I love to work with people who are interested in what they are doing. It doesn't need to be so ready and so perfect. I am not perfect. I think that the worker must be satisfied. That is the most important thing. Then it comes, if it comes.

Is the teamwork very important to you?
I love it. Teamwork is important: that people feel 'I am with you and I give something to this thing'. When everybody wants to help, it blossoms. And good luck is very important too. And a good feeling. If the process is positive, then it can succeed.

Someone told me you once said: 'I only wish God would create one more basic form.' Is that true?
Oh yes, yes. Because the cylinder is excellent, the ball is excellent and many other forms. But they have been copied and used so many times that I want God to make a new one. But this has not happened.

When people talk about what Finnish design is, they often mention you in their explanation. But what do you think Finnish design is? How would you describe it?
Finnish design is all that is not me, that is not here, but it is the sum of the details. There are some who think they know what Finnish design is, but it is not that way. It is a mix of many things.

Toikka expresses himself honestly in his work and in conversation too. His influential charm has helped him in his collaborative work, not least with the glass-blowers he relies on to articulate his ideas. The Great Horned Owl Uhuu, is a favourite piece from his Birds collection.

The Barn Owl and Little Barn Owl are among the most characterful of Toikka's Birds.

SKILLS AND TRADITIONS

My way is that I don't make drawings. I go there and we talk and talk.

OIVA TOIKKA

Left
Toikka has worked in close collaboration with the glass-blowers of Nuutajärvi throughout his career. During the 1970s he hit his stride and became more and more experimental, using his accumulated knowledge in increasingly inventive ways.

Above
Toikka's first bird was Flycatcher 1971. Such early examples were later relaunched with a commercial ambition in 1994. Toikka has designed more than 400 birds in total.

Above
Techniques that are particular to Nuutajärvi have been exploited and manipulated to great effect by Toikka throughout his career. For example, strands of glass and oxides have been cleverly used to represent feathering on the Birds.

Right
Since 1977, Toikka has produced an Annual Art Object for Iittala. These collectible cubes are miniature, captured worlds, made with great care and precision. Ever resourceful, Toikka makes use of the rejects from this project in large-scale installations.

The colours and playfulness of the Lollipop works and Pompom vases of the 1960s were a purposeful reference to the pop art of the time. The Lollipop work above is from 1969.

> **There are some who think they know what Finnish design is, but it is not that way. It is a mix of many things.**
>
> OIVA TOIKKA

Trees Reflected in a Lake 1972 is a technically brilliant work, typically experimental and representive of the symbolism and sense of composition in Toikka's ambitious artworks.

Kari Virtanen prefers to be called a cabinet-maker rather than a designer: he believes that it describes much better the intuitive and time-honoured woodworking skills for which he is known. But while Virtanen may consider himself a humble craftsman, his admirers and collaborators include some of the greatest names in Finnish culture. For example, he has worked with Alvar Aalto, Yrjö Kukkapuro and Kaj Franck.

Through his company, Nikari, he produces crafted furniture for a mass audience while also taking on individual commissions. Virtanen also shares his knowledge with a new generation of makers at Aalto University. While he uses traditional methods, he is no relic from the past. He calls his Fiskars workshop a 'lab' and is adept at streamlining processes and exploring future, ecological uses of wood, the material he is so closely associated with.

WOOD WORKS
KARI VIRTANEN

Virtanen's workshop in Fiskars is ideally placed: he selects his timber by choosing trees from the forest around him, which are then felled and cut at the local saw mill.

Did you begin working with wood at a young age?
Before I was old enough to go to school, I would make porridge whisks from pine branches. I have rather humble roots. I was the eldest of four children and needed to earn some money for the family. But there was a passion too. I became an apprentice at a carpenter's workshop when I was 14. When I was 19, I established a workshop in Seinäjoki, which I have now been running for 45 years. I did everything at a very young age, including having two daughters in my twenties. I've also always provided work for other people.

How have things changed since then?
I began by making period furniture in baroque, classical and other styles. I realised that each period needs its individual style. An understanding of different periods is still useful for my product design.

What made you come to Fiskars?
I relocated here more than 20 years ago, as all of my clients are in southern Finland. However, it was the unique forest nature in Fiskars that was the deciding factor. The area boasts vast woodlands and about 30 different types of trees, including all the main species of hardwood. The raw materials are right on my doorstep, which is increasingly important, as we specialise in local production. The Nikari workshop in Fiskars has Finland's most prominent sawmill for speciality wood.

> # Designers carry a responsibility: they need to design products that create work.
>
> KARI VIRTANEN

You want to hold on to the title of cabinet-maker. What is your attitude towards design?
I've never wanted to call myself a designer. The valuable craftsmanship of a cabinet-maker serves as my starting point. Years ago, Kaj Franck visited my workshop when I was already working on my own collection of pine stools, tables and other furniture. When Kaj commented on their good design, I didn't really know what he meant. He encouraged me to get involved in design, seeing that I had an aesthetic eye and a desire to create from my own starting points.

How long does a project normally take you to complete?
I take a long time to process things, such as reflecting on the qualities of wooden furniture in the future. A completely new universal design language is required. Speed is an important element in the future, which can be achieved through craftsmanship. At best, we have managed to create prototypes within four hours. Extremely efficient product development is one of Nikari's strengths. I'm familiar with all the manufacturing techniques and equipment, and know how the job can be done. Products that are challenging to make are something of a narcissistic icon for a designer. Designers carry a responsibility: they need to design products that create work.

Is there a type of wood you enjoy working with the most?
It always depends on what we are producing at the time. At the moment, I want to create a more delicate, fine and elegant finish, which has led me to use ash. The material shouldn't really make any difference. Outstanding quality and design come first.

When are you satisfied with your work?
I'm never totally satisfied, and the satisfaction from finishing something lasts no more than five minutes. I love the creative process and always keep a distance from the finished product. As grim as it may sound, I've received the most positive feedback for coffins. I've created coffins for a number of important Finnish designers.

Is there a product you would like to create but haven't yet had the opportunity to?
I always have some crazy ideas tucked away. For a long time I thought about making the world's finest pipes. Now I love the idea of creating storage solutions, which is a world of its own. I have, in fact, made some nice cupboards, and this area continues to fascinate me. I'm also interested in making bows and arrows, and the next project is to create a wooden bathtub for a private residence.

Any particular cause that is close to your heart?
Sustainable forest growth. Forest plunder is unfathomable. Nature is designed to be wasteful. After all, a single spruce produces five million seeds, only 10 of which generate a new tree. And plenty of bilberries get left in the forest every year. The pulp industry isn't doing too well, which allows us to generate new ways of making use of forests. Xylitol is a good example of using wood in a novel way and I'm sure other similar innovations will arise. Trees continue to hold a great deal of research potential.

The details in Virtanen's designs are born from function. Specialist joints allow the wood to move as it gathers moisture or dries out—a necessity in Finland's varying climate.

The material shouldn't really make any difference. Outstanding quality and design come first.
KARI VIRTANEN

This page
The restored original floor of the workshop is made from solid wooden blocks.

Left
There aren't too many machines in Virtanen's workshop: as much as possible is made by hand. Virtanen also prefers to sketch by hand because 'the flow is more creative'.

Ceramicist Nathalie Lahdenmäki's tableware is designed to optimise and celebrate the craft methods of making that are so integral to their appeal. The resulting vessels are irregular in shape, delicate in appearance and purposefully tactile.

Lahdenmäki has collaborated with Arabia and Iittala since graduating in 1999 from the University of Art and Design Helsinki, which has since merged with Aalto University, where she is also now a lecturer. But her true spirit is expressed in her studio work, driven by the desire to sustain the joy of hand-making.

A CAREFUL CRAFT
NATHALIE LAHDENMÄKI

How did you become a ceramist?
I've loved to draw and paint since I was little, and I always knew I wanted to work in the field of art. I dreamt of becoming an illustrator. I went to an arts-oriented senior secondary school, where my ceramics teacher told me I should apply to the University of Art and Design Helsinki [now Aalto University]. It happened by chance, but I have no regrets. Ceramics swept me away.

When did you start to feel established?
I started teaching as soon as I graduated when I was 25. At the same time, I established my own studio and began to work. Teaching has been important to me. It initially provided me with a living and has supported my own work. I was rather brave and hard-working in the beginning and believed in what I was doing. Since then, both collaboration with industry and working on my own pieces have continued.

What qualities characterise your work?
I focus strongly on texture. My own pieces reflect the fact that they aren't mass-produced. This can be done by creating thin sides or asymmetric forms, or by allowing the piece to take a life of its own in the kiln. I'm fascinated by the interplay of matt and shiny surfaces. It all comes down to rather subtle elements.

What influences your choice of colours?
Intuition. I've been working on my colour palette for years and I'm quite satisfied. At one point, I veered towards greys that shifted towards black. Before that I used a lot of pastels. Pink has stayed with me all along, which is a rather atypical hue for ceramics. The latest colour I wanted to throw in was bright yellow. Adding the desired shade to the glaze is hard work, so there's no point changing too early on.

Where do you find inspiration for new pieces in your own collection?
My own collection began with just one cup, but has been growing ever since. A new product may be inspired by a particularly fascinating form. In other words, I proceed in a rather unsystematic way. I add one or two pieces to my collection each year, slowly but surely.

Where do you draw your energy from for developing something new?
I've often thought that I could happily delegate moulding and other rather monotonous stages to someone else. But now I've come to realise that it's the most important stage and so I want to do it myself.

I'm rather careful and contemplative, and having to constantly create something new would be exhausting. I enjoy walking, visiting deserted places, going to the mountains and trekking. People often ask me where I find inspiration, but it's more a question of how to empty my thoughts. An empty mind creates room for something new.

Does a Finnish design philosophy affect what you do?
Finnish design places value on everyday, practical objects: their functionality and simple forms. Although I appreciate these qualities, I'm mostly interested in aesthetics. My theory is that if you like something, you end up using it. You learn to live with objects you love, like holding a cup without a handle. There's a myriad of products because there are so many different types of people.

Is there any particular cause that is close to your heart?
Perhaps it's unfashionable to talk about handicraft, but I think it has a special value. People need to maintain the ability to feel and work with their hands, and not just with their minds.

> # People need to maintain the ability to feel and work with their hands, and not just with their minds.
>
> NATHALIE LAHDENMÄKI

Lahdenmäki's studio works are the result of a subtle play between shape, colour and texture. Just a handful of new pieces are added to the collection each year, allowing it to evolve slowly and purposefully.

PTÁCI NASLOUCHAJÍ ZPĚVU VÄINEMÖINENOVU

When talking about Finnish national identity, mention of The Kalevala is never far away. First published in 1845, this epic poem by Elias Lönnrot is regarded as the epitome of Finnish literature, capturing and defining the national character, landscape and psyche. It made a key contribution to the growing sense of nationality which led to Finland's independence from Russia in 1917.

The story is a compilation of ancient folklore tales that were originally sung. They tell of heroes and villains, mythical creatures, journeys, tests and trials. Today, The Kalevala remains an effective touchstone for Finland's creatives and an inspiration for those in search of the essence of Finnishness.

MYTH MAKING
THE KALEVALA

THUS THE ANCIENT VÄINÄMÖINEN, IN HIS COPPER-BANDED VESSEL, LEFT HIS TRIBE IN KALEVALA, SAILING O'ER THE ROLLING BILLOWS, SAILING THROUGH THE AZURE VAPORS, SAILING THROUGH THE DUSK OF EVENING, SAILING TO THE FIERY SUNSET, TO THE HIGHER-LANDED REGIONS, TO THE LOWER VERGE OF HEAVEN…

CANTO 50, LINE 493

Right
The Kalevala Series of annual limited edition plates was produced by Arabia between 1976 and 1999. Designer Raija Uosikkinen's motifs each depict a story from the national epic, an extract from which is written on the reverse of the plates in Finnish, Swedish and English.

The Kalevala was written during the Romantic period in Finland when there was much emphasis on establishing a national identity and the Finnish language itself was still fledgling. Lönnrot was a physician, botanist and linguist. His sweeping epic is made up of material gathered during numerous field trips to Karelia and eastern Finland. References from The Kalevala quickly became motifs during the Romantic period: names were lifted and given to places and companies and visual cues were applied to buildings and objects. The story was illustrated and reprinted many times.

The version best known today consists of 22,795 verses, divided into 50 songs, or cantos. It has since been retold by many artists in many styles, perhaps most famously by Akseli Gallén-Kallela. Lönnrot's work influenced J.R.R. Tolkien and inspired the music of composer Jean Sibelius. The story remains a potent cultural force today, particularly in Finland, where it is frequently referenced in design, music and art. Indeed, its cultural reach is so broad it seems to influence just about everything, from a Kalevala-themed Donald Duck cartoon to tattoo designs to ice-cream flavours.

Below, right and following page
Illustrator Stanislav Kolíbal's interpretation of The Kalevala is very different to the ornate depictions that came before. His illustrations were first published in 1962 in a book by author Vladislav Stanovský.

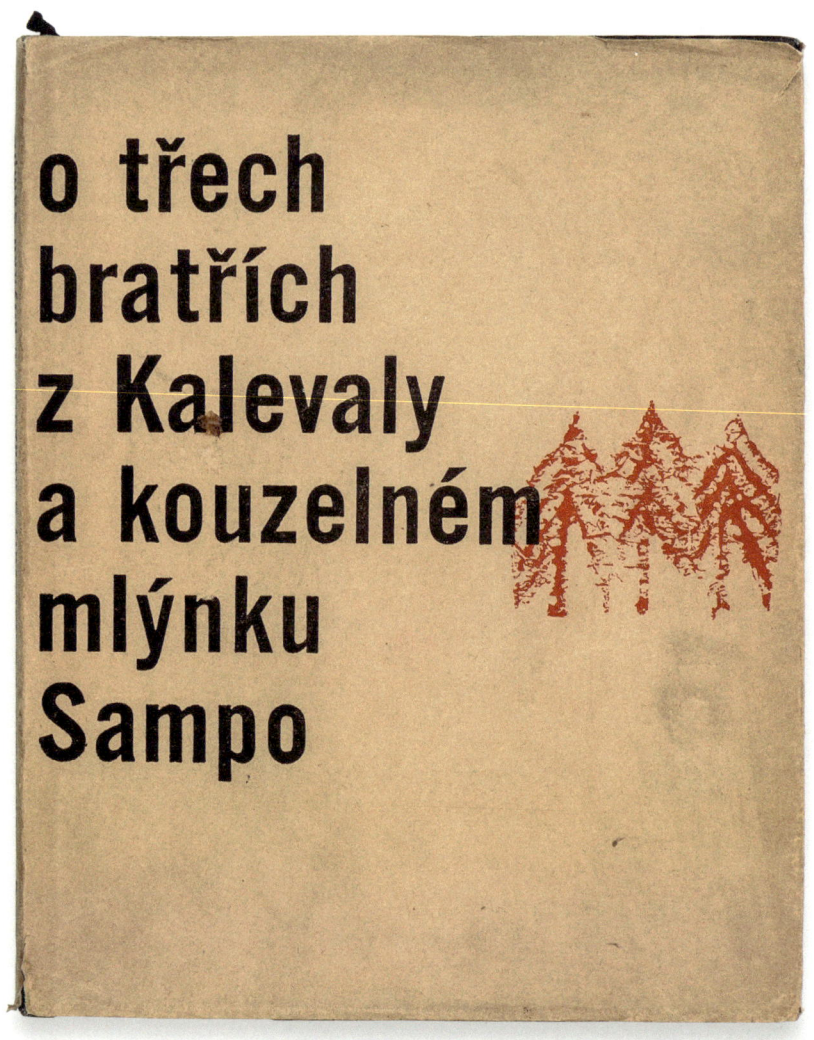

OZBROJENCI KRÁLOVNY LOUHI

Tři bratři odnesou mlýnek Sampo

Už svítalo a slunce se soukalo do světnice, když Väinemöinen dopil poslední džbán do dna a pravil:
„Mocná královno, ukaž nám aspoň na chvilku, jak mlýnek Sampo mele mouku, sůl a zlato. Rádi bychom se na něj aspoň podívali."
Královna Louhi odpověděla:
„To se může stát. Ale nemyslete si, že se vám podaří mlýnek odnést. Hlídá ho tisíc ozbrojenců. A i kdybyste přemohli tisíc ozbrojenců, nepřemůžete psa Halliho a fenu Lukki. A i kdybyste přemohli psa Halliho a fenu Lukki, mne nepřemůžete. Však to sami dobře víte."
Pak zavedla královna Louhi tři bratry do velikánské světnice, ne ve svém hradu dřevěném, ne ve svém hradu kostěném, ale ve svém hradu kamenném, na sedm zámků zamčeném, a tam stálo tisíc ozbrojenců a hlídal pes Halli a fena Lukki kouzelný mlýnek Sampo. Stál tam, celý ze zlata na stříbrném stole, jedním složením mlel mouku, druhým sůl a třetím zlato. A neustále přicházeli a odcházeli sluhové a odnášeli pytle mouky, soli a zlata pryč.
Královna Louhi pyšně pohlédla na to bohatství a zazpívala píseň:

„Nikde jinde na světě
štěstí lidem nekvete
jako u nás v Pohjole,
v Pohjole, ó v Pohjole.
Jsou tu domy z pecnů chleba,
střechy z bílých koláčů,
stromy jsou tu plné šunek,
s pečení pekáčů.
V řekách plavou pěkné ryby,
vařené i smažené,

v potocích se pění pivo,
věřte mi to nebo ne,
ale nikde na světě
štěstí lidem nekvete
jako v pyšné Pohjole,
v Pohjole, ó v Pohjole.
Místo kamení jsou sýry,
místo bláta máslo je,
v polích tady rostou sukně,
kalhoty a košile.

Tři bratři odnesou mlýnek Sampo 69

Zaradoval se Väinemöinen:
„Dobře, že jsem tě, loďko, našel. Už nebudeš hnít ve vodě, větry ti nebudou rvát červenou plachtu, ptáci ti nebudou hnízda stavět na stožáru a pod tvým kýlem se nebudou prohánět protivné rybky. Vypluju s tebou na širé moře za nevěstou do pusté Pohjoly, do temné Tapioly, pro dceru mocné královny Louhi."
A pak napjal Väinemöinen červenou plachtu na opuštěné lodi a vítr ho zahnal na modré moře. Cestou se ještě zastavil u matky Iroi, aby se s ní rozloučil.
Stála matka Iroi na břehu, dívala se na modré moře, dívala se, divila se:
„Copak se to tam tak červená na modrém moři? Je-li to ryba, proč se nepotopí ve vodě? Je-li to pták, proč nevzlétí do oblak? Je-li to Väinemöinenova loď, ať se obrátí přídí ke mně a kormidlem do cizí země."
Väinemöinen přistál u břehu a matka Iroi se ho zeptala:
„Kampak máš, synku, namířeno?"
„Jedu do Laponska lovit lososy, matko."
„Když můj tatíček jezdil lovit lososy, měl plnou loď sítí, na sítích plno nevodů, pod sítěmi dlouhá bidla. Ale ty máš jen svoje kantele."
„Jedu do Ladogy lovit labutě, matko."
„Když můj tatíček jezdil lovit labutě, měl na zádech luk, u pasu toulec na šípy a u nohou smečku psů. A ty máš jenom svoje kantele."
„Jedu, matko, do pusté Pohjoly, do temné Tapioly, za nevěstou, dcerou mocné královny Louhi."
Zarazila se matka Iroi, ale syna nijak nezrazovala.
„Jeď si, synku! Dcera královny Louhi je krásná jako slunce, ale královna Louhi je zlá jako noc, která slunce z nebe zahání. Je to divoká země, tam bohatýry jedí a topí v moři. Dej si dobrý pozor. Jsi moudrý, snad si dobře povede."
A tak odjel Väinemöinen do temné Pohjoly za nevěstou.

20 Väinemöinen se vypraví za nevěstou na lodi

ILMARINEN ODJÍŽDÍ ZA NEVĚSTOU

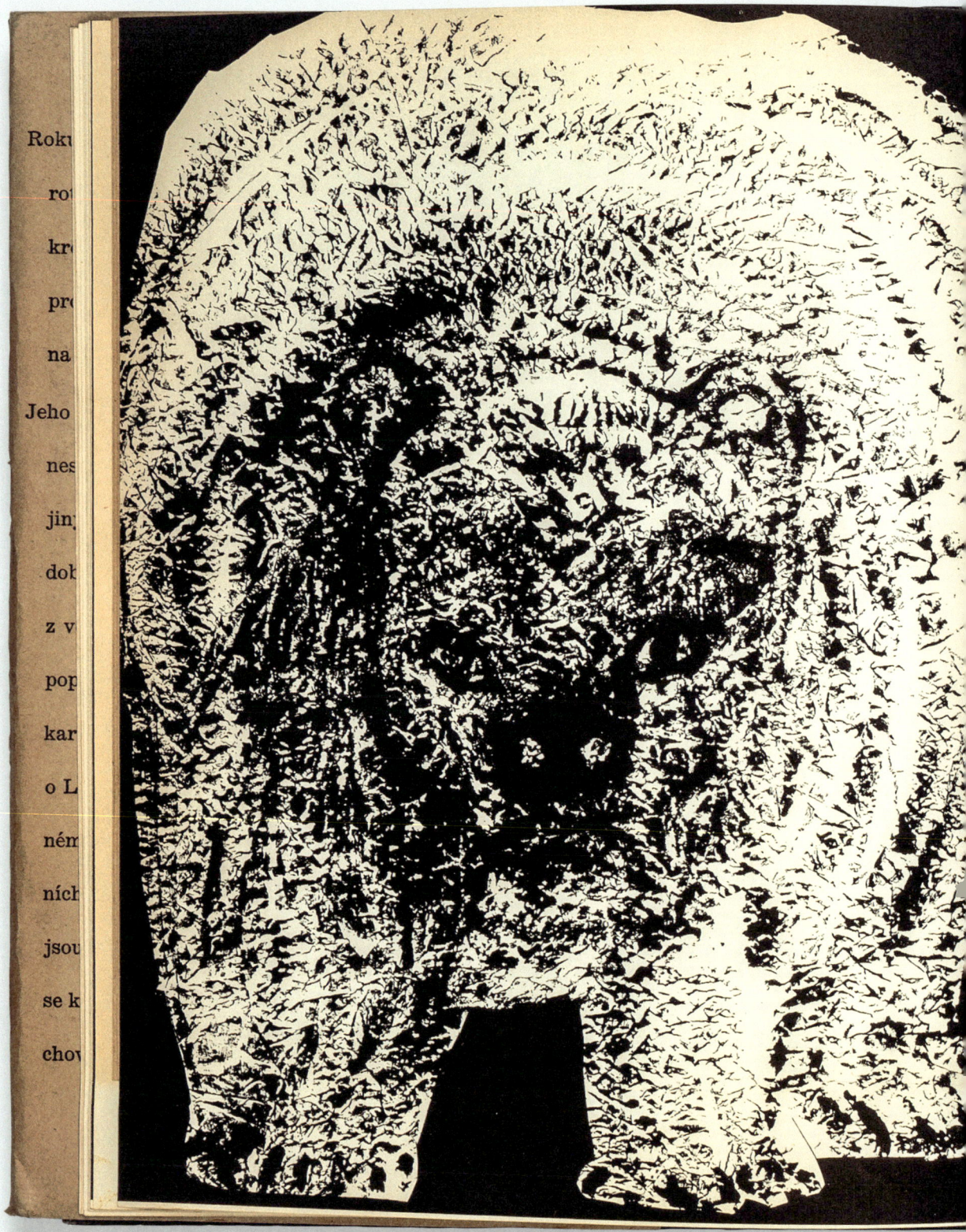

Roku

rot

kre

pro

na

Jeho

nes

jin

dob

z v

pop

kar

o L

ném

ních

jsou

se k

chov

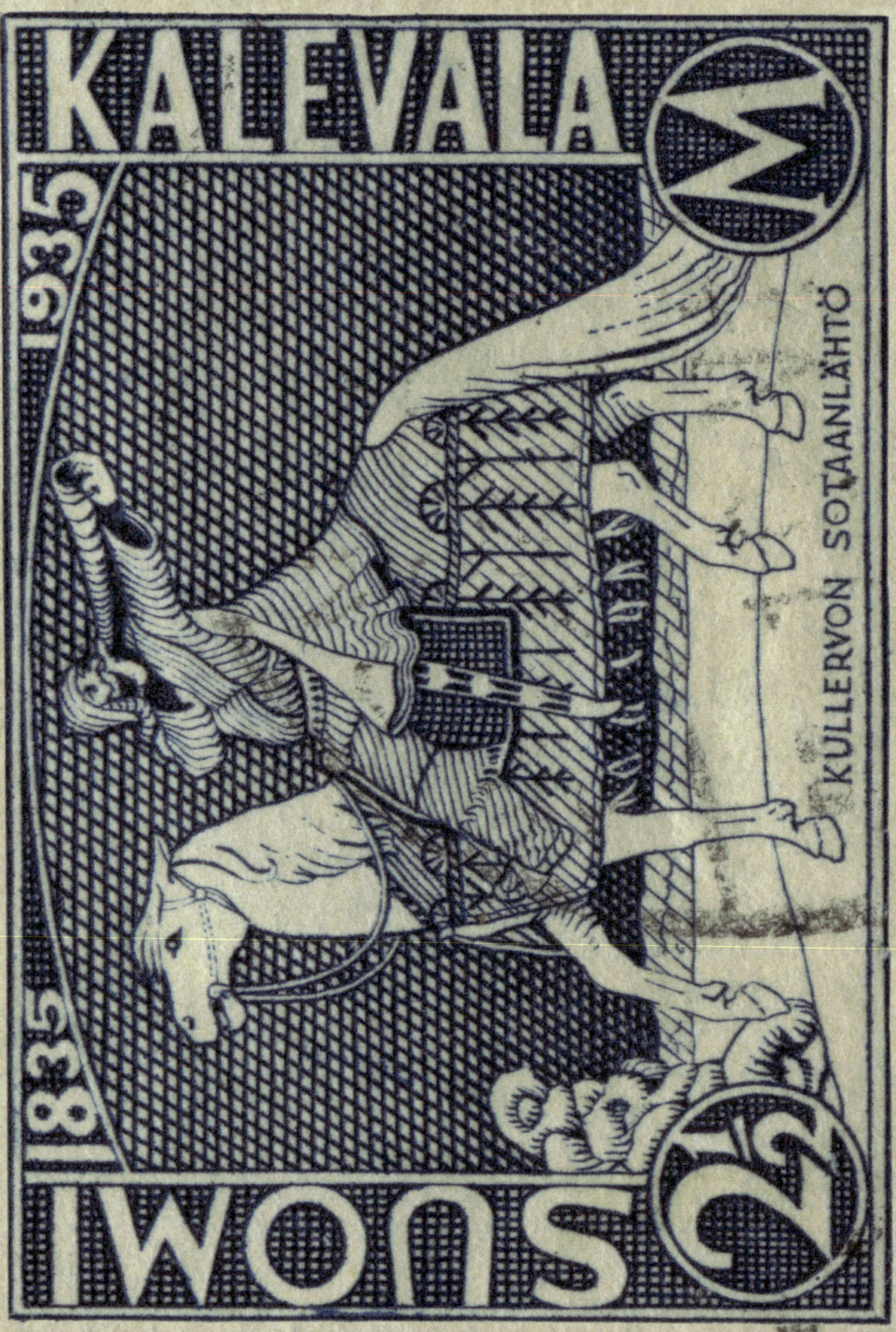

Imagery from The Kalevala has long been pervasive in Finland. Its characters and motifs have appeared on many everyday items, such as these commemorative centenary postage stamps from 1935 with illustrations including those of Akseli Gallen-Kallela.

Today, the Finnish illustrator and designer Klaus Haapaniemi lives in London. But the influence of his homeland's landscape and imagery remains potent in his work, perhaps even more so because he is now further away from it. 'Somehow when you're living abroad it gets stronger,' he says.

Detailed ornate illustration from Russian folklore is the inspiration for his drawings which adorn everything from ceramics to textiles. His work is much in demand: he has recently opened a flagship store, is designing for several international retailers and working on a project with the Finnish National Opera.

A MAGICAL PLAYGROUND
KLAUS HAAPANIEMI

How did your design career begin?
I actually studied graphic design, illustration and design. I freelanced for a few years in Helsinki and after that I became part of a design agency—that was in Helsinki too. And then I moved to Italy to work for a fashion company as a print designer. But I got really tired of fashion, so I moved to London four years later. After the fashion period, I was interested in interiors and textiles.

Your style is distinctive. When did that emerge? Or did it evolve?
I was simultaneously working with different styles 10 or 15 years ago. It's hard to describe how it happens, but I think this style is very natural to me. It reflects my background from Finland and all the things I've seen.

The history of storytelling and narrative is very rich in Finland. Is that an influence?
Yeah, it is. If you compare it to Scandinavian design especially, it's very different because it's so detailed. People tend to think that the Finnish design is part of the Scandinavian minimalist tradition. But there is this other side, because Finland is so close to Russia. My style is more from that side, I think.

I've looked at many great Russian artists and illustrators and experienced that world quite a lot. When I was growing up in Finland, it was all over books, television and everywhere. Ivan Bilibin was one of the greatest inspirations when I was growing up: I read a lot of his books. I still collect books by Russian illustrators. It's the style that interests me, the hand-drawn delicate style.

And The Kalevala is taught to you in school isn't it, in Finland?
Yes. I have never read the book, but in school we were taught parts of it. Tolkien was interested in it when he wrote his books. And I think the mythological part is really close to me. What I think of life, and how I see the British culture and nature, is part of that.

Is the inspiration as strong for you now, even though you live elsewhere?
Somehow when you're living abroad it gets stronger.

Are you telling stories with your illustrations?
I think people tend to see them as that. But it's more like a theme: it's not really storytelling for me. I think in products the story should be quite abstract. The theme shouldn't be too underlined.

You've worked recently with some traditional Finnish crafts, such as ryjjy rugs…
I approached the Friends Of Finnish Handicraft. I have wanted to work with them for a long time and the Finnish government gave us some money for a project. I made just one piece, and it's more like an art piece. I think it's more than 4.5 metres wide and maybe 1.5 or 2 metres tall, so it's a really large piece. It is a very traditional craft in Finland and the Friends of Finnish Handicraft are really quite famous for their skills. There's lots of talent there.

Is there any other craft process that is interesting to you?
Most of our products, our own products, are made in India. They are totally handmade, handprinted or handsewn and embroidered, so it's really important for me that our products stand in that position in the market.

Your work is very decorative, very emotive. There aren't many people who follow the path you've chosen.
There are more nowadays. I see now that some young people are more interested in decorative arts. I think the trend nowadays is more for modern Scandinavian style, without any patterns or decorations, but still I think there is interest in decoration too.

Finland is a new country, and craft tradition and heritage are perhaps not that far away: they are not so much a part of the distant past as they are elsewhere.
I guess it is a little bit similar in England. There is such a big respect for craft and artists like William Morris, for example, who was a part of that global movement in the nineteenth century. One other artist and designer that I greatly respect is Josef Frank who was designing for Swedish companies like Svenskt Tenn. He was living at exactly the same time as William Morris and there were lots of influences back and forth. You can see at the same time they are really modern, but there is tradition too and it is really quite humorous. William Morris's design compared to Josef Frank, it was a bit more serious.

They both used natural motifs a lot. Is that an inspiration for you too?
That's a really big inspiration, especially the techniques that William Morris used. He used log printing and natural dyed colours from plants and was really against using leads and metallic colours. So I think that is really interesting and also part of this time, where people are wondering what to do next. I wouldn't say that it's the only way to do it, but there's a point and relevance to it. Because the printing industry nowadays is almost totally based in China. But I guess there are other techniques.

Your visual language appeals to lots of different countries. But do people in Finland understand it on a different level, do you think?
Yes. It's much easier for them to understand it, but maybe the younger generation not so much. They don't know the background so well, but people my age know exactly.

Do you sketch? Do you work on a computer or by hand?
I use all kinds of methods available. It's more idea-based. When I get an idea on an aeroplane or train or wherever, then I need to remember it, so I sketch on paper. But I use computers for executing the final idea, print or illustration.

Your collection for Iittala brought you to a large audience.
It seemed a really easy decision to work with them. The products come with many kind of patterns already, but I guess it really freshened up their image. I think I made three different printed collections for Iittala and I've been designing a glass collection for them too.

What do you think about those cornerstones of Finnish design: ceramic, glass, textiles. I guess you've kind of touched on all of those really…
I haven't yet worked for Artek. That's something that I'd really love to do.

The Hel Yes! event was a great project. Whose idea was that?
The original idea was ours, but the Finnish Institute in London commissioned us to do the project. That's how we got the funding. We wanted to work together on the tables and with Antto [Melasniemi]. We had similar kinds of intentions, and that whole fusion of food and design and art… You never know what happens in that kind of process. It's kind of improvised.

Right
Klaus Haapaniemi and Mia Wallenius.

Bottom right
The Golden Owl.

Bottom left
Haapaniemi created a limited edition label for Koskenkorva Vodka First Harvest 2010, which was served at one of the Hel Yes! events in 2012. 'The theme springs from a romanticised image of Finnish marine trading and travelling,' says Haapaniemi.

Noel Russo print.

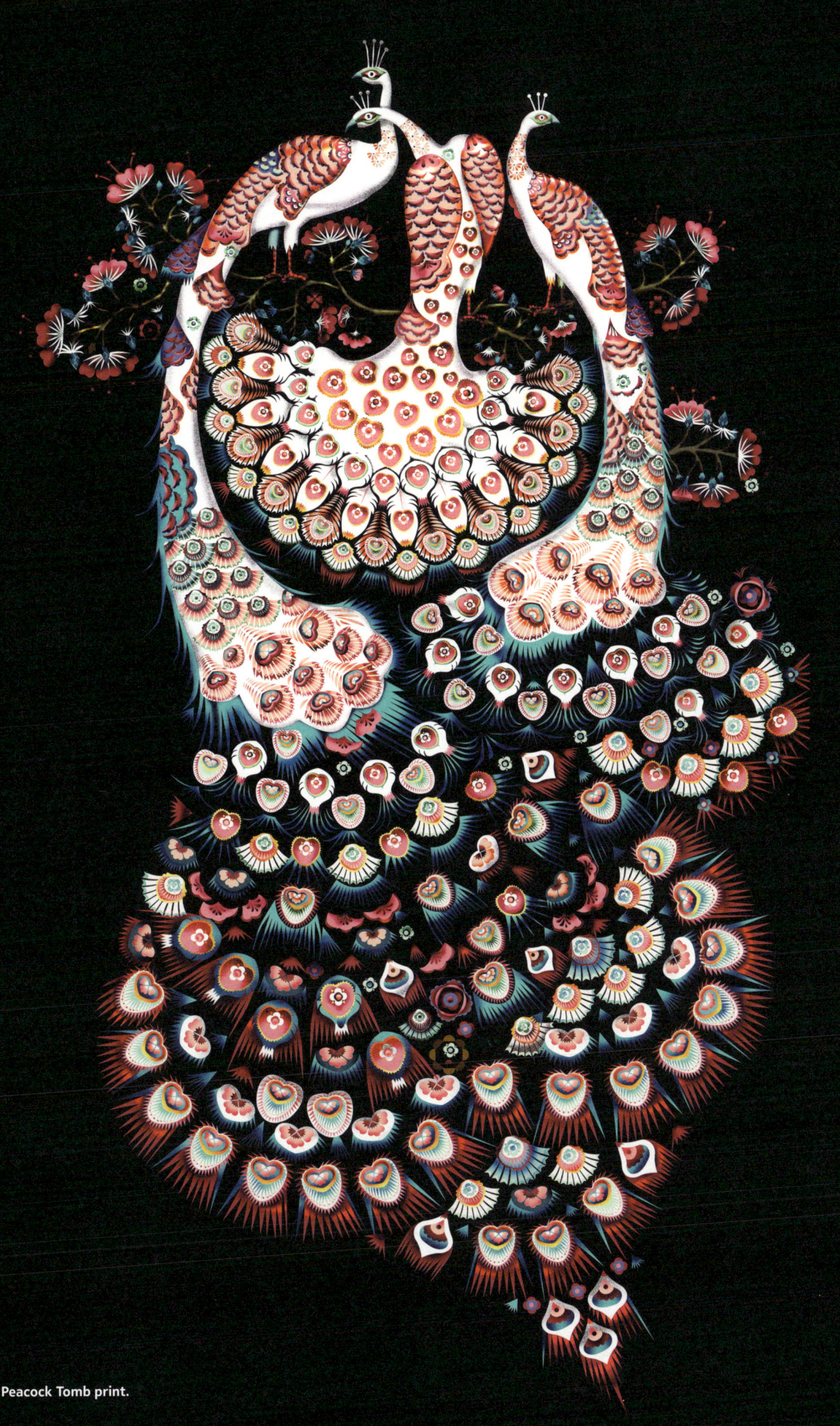

Peacock Tomb print.

SKILLS AND TRADITIONS

Ivan Bilibin was one of the greatest inspirations when I was growing up: I read a lot of his books. I still collect books by Russian illustrators. It's the hand-drawn delicate style that interests me.

KLAUS HAAPANIEMI

Above
Watercolour sketches are part of his repertoire.

Left
Work for Isetan, a department store in Tokyo.

For more than 40 years, Fujiwo Ishimoto has used textile and ceramic design to articulate his observations of nature, his love of graphic form and his dexterity with colour and pattern. Although Ishimoto moved to Helsinki from Tokyo in 1970 he is, by his own admission, 'very Japanese'. And yet his evocative, lyrical works that speak so much about landscape and seasons have earned their place as iconic Finnish designs.

Perhaps more than any other designer, Ishimoto represents the somewhat mythical cultural connection between Japan and Finland. Ishimoto counts Oiva Toikka among his closest friends and he has worked with Kaj Franck at the Arabia factory where he has kept a studio on the ninth floor for many years. He also once travelled 600 kilometres across the length of his adopted homeland by bicycle.

THE QUIET MAN
FUJIWO ISHIMOTO

Why did you first come to Helsinki?
The mood in Japan in the 1960s was to travel. Also, I was very unsatisfied. I worked in Japan for six years in marketing and graphic design, not product design. I was working for a textile company, making catalogues and invitations, and also displays and shop design. I specialized in designing kimono shops.

But my interest was very much in Finland, which I knew about through magazines. At the end of the 1960s, I saw the work of avant-garde designers such as Eero Aarnio in Tokyo. And even at the beginning of the 1960s, I was aware of Marimekko, which was very modern and exciting. My teacher recommended that I think about textile design.

And did you?
No. I didn't think it was very exciting. But maybe the teacher saw something in me: a special feeling for colour, touch, or colour combinations and so on. I went from the countryside to Tokyo after high school. And then I wanted to go to a national art university, but it was very competitive and I thought: 'This is impossible! I'm a mere country boy; I can't do this.' So I went to a school that helped you get in and I was very lucky: our teacher was brilliant. I did graphic design and sculpture, and my colour scheme was something different. I was accepted.

When you came to Helsinki, you met Armi Ratia at Marimekko. Is that right?
Yes. I asked if it was possible for me to work there and to produce textile designs. I had never done it before. It was quite funny. I only had some graphic work: one book that I had done. She was interested and asked the director, but there was nothing at that moment for me. Then I met Ristomatti Ratia, Armi Ratia's son, who ran a sister company called Décembre. I began working for him, making graphics and displays and shooting photography and product designs. I did everything, even painted walls.

You were a labourer too?
I had never done such work in Japan. So I learnt a lot of things. But I had time to think of my own ideas too. I saw an article about a small Polish village and found some of the rough wall paintings there interesting. Marimekko was intrigued and sent me to tale a closer look. They paid for my trip.

And your first design came from that?
I drew the pattern. I didn't paint it. I didn't believe my brush work was comparable to Maija Isola or Katsuji Wakisaka, the other two designers at Marimekko then. I didn't have any technique. They are more technically minded and I'm not. So I just started with ideas.

The end result was Kuja 1976. It's very beautiful.
Then I passed the Marimekko exam.

You went on to produce collections of quiet designs such as Mättäillä.
Which is still selling! For more than 20 years now.

Was that collection very much inspired by landscape? Is nature your most common inspiration?
Yes: what is happening in nature.

Is it a Finnish landscape or a Japanese landscape?
It is only in my head. There are no clouds so blue. It is a fantasy.

The colours you use in your textiles and ceramics are very special. Is the palette always from your imagination?
I usually create with no colour, just shape. At that stage I don't have any colour sense. Then I apply the colour as another stage. I don't know where they come from, the colours. Some are natural colours and some are more artistic—my interpretation. And people like it more that way, in my experience. I have, not a thousand, maybe just 20 colours in my palette. That's how to create. So it is quite limited. But how they work is in the combination, how they overlap and, with ceramics, how they work on different clay.

I wanted to ask you about the relationship between Japan and Finland. Are there similarities, especially when it comes to the influence of nature on designers such as yourself?
But nature is everywhere: in Germany and in England too. Japan has a completely different landscape. It's very different to Finnish landscapes.

When you won the Kaj Franck prize, you designed a poster that showed two stones. Can you tell me about that image?
I was in Japan that year. The first stone is from a Shinto shrine. I saw that it had been put there or maybe someone had found it there and just cleaned it up. When I came back to Finland, I went to Lapland and there I saw these different stones. The first stone was quite Japanese; the other was very Finnish. That's why I put the two together.

I think it's the perfect description of the two cultures. There's an essence that's the same, but they are different too: the first is slightly more refined and the second is raw. Do you return to Japan often?
Nowadays yes, once a year. But previously not so often. I left in 1970 and 1974 was the first time I returned. Then I went back again in 1981.

Top left
The poster Ishimoto created to advertise his Kaj Franck prize exhibition.

Clockwise from top right
Working with ceramic allows Ishimoto a creative freedom he enjoys. He makes full use of the technical capacity of the Arabia factory to use his latest material in ever-expressive ways. The depiction of nature remains his concern and he employs glazes to represent soil, melting snow and water.

> I like to do handiwork myself; to make something myself.
> FUJIWO ISHIMOTO

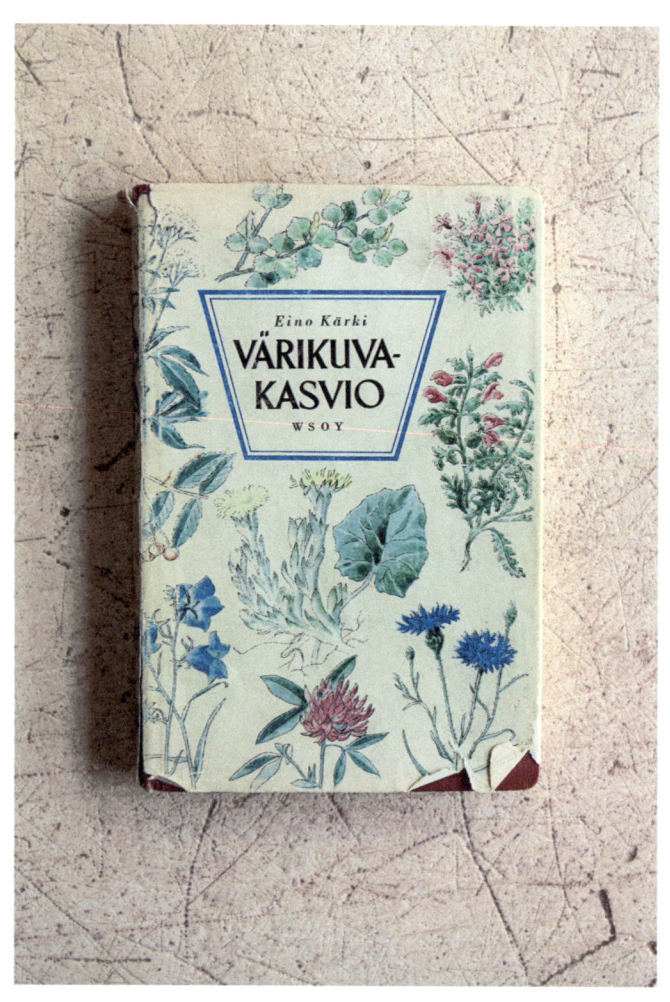

Flowers is Ishimoto's latest collection of works. Finnish wild flowers are reimagined and turned into wall-mounted motifs. Well-worn reference books and a multitude of sketches and glaze samples litter the Arabia studio Ishimoto has inhabited for many years.

> # I don't know where they come from, the colours.
>
> FUJIWO ISHIMOTO

When you first came here, was it a culture shock?
It wasn't a shock because I admired it. I had first gone to New York but I already knew everything about it from TV in Japan. But in Finland, everything was so fresh to me.

What was Helsinki like then?
The city was not yet developed. There were lots of empty spaces. I liked it. It had something: the city had some shadows. Nowadays that is no more: everything is new and full. It can't be helped. She's grown up: it's normal. But in 1970, everything was very clean and silent and people were very friendly. You see, when I first came here I was still undecided whether to stay. But I remember a man coming over and hugging me saying 'Japanese'! He was quite drunk, I think.

But the Finnish were happy to see you!
They were very warm.

Helsinki is a city that is very close to nature; close to the water and close to the country. Was that useful for you, for your inspiration?
Yes. Even in the city nature is close. And I don't have a summer house. I don't have a car.

I read that you once cycled across Finland.
I once rode to the north in three weeks, by bicycle.

How long did you spend designing fabrics for Marimekko?
From 1974 to 2006. I made over 300 prints—400, I think.

Is there one collection that was your favourite?
If I pick one, I always pick the Mättäillä collection. And I always use this collection. My tablecloth is always this.

Designs such as these are subtle, and not what some might associate with Finnish prints from the period.
This is what I am interested in—not shouting. I like quiet.

When did you begin to make ceramics?
In 1989, here at Arabia, as a scholarship. I decided I could try it and they gave me a lot of help.

How long have you been producing the Flower collection?
I began hanging them in the corridors here in 2000 and nobody was interested. Finally someone noticed them and bought one. Then, for a summer exhibition called Garden, I made 15 flowers and hung them on the walls. They immediately sold out and they wanted me to make more.

What is the appeal of ceramics for you?
It's very interesting, very exciting. Because I like to do handiwork myself; to make something myself. I enjoy that. If I just draw it and someone else makes it, that could be much better—that's art. But I'm not interested in that. I am limited by what I can do myself and that is good.

Rut Bryk started out as a graphic designer and before that she had dreamt of becoming an architect. However, she was destined to become an artist, choosing ceramics as her method of expression. Yet the three-dimensional spaces and expansive metropolis-like panoramas of her later works reveal that those early influences never really left her.

Bryk went to work at the Arabia factory in 1942, out of leaving college, and stayed there until the end of her career in the 1990s. Her work has been exhibited worldwide and her monumental pieces are integral to important architectural projects such as the Helsinki City Hall and the Mäntyniemi Residence of the President of Finland.

THE EYE THAT TRAVELS
RUT BRYK

Rut Bryk's early work was influenced by her mentors at Arabia: it was decorative; naïvely illustrative. An underlying romanticism and love of storytelling remained in her work as it grew increasingly abstract throughout her career. Geometric patterns and spatial reliefs—a new decorative language—emerged in the 1960s. Her works became constructs, complex and intriguing. The wall reliefs that came to characterise her work are unique landscapes, at once foreign, yet familiar.

Travel to faraway places like India inspired Bryk, as did the work of artists like Matisse and Vasarely. She called her husband, Tapio Wirkkala, her 'most important critic' and together they explored natural landscapes, using the endless inspiration it provided in their work. At the end of her career, she was creating ever-more ambitious artworks, some reaching 30 metres in length, each constructed from thousands of individual tiles. Her work remains unique, unsurpassed, and an example of how decorative art can be bent into something remarkable by strength of character and imagination alone.

Top right
Bryk's larger wall reliefs, such as Kaupunki Veden Äärellä (City by the Water) 1982, would be laid out horizontally on the floor of a studio and she would view them from the top of a ladder. The giant commissions were often destined for official buildings in Finland and across the world.

Bottom right
This giant installation, Kaupunki Auringossa (City in the Sun) 1975, is a feature in the Helsinki City Hall.

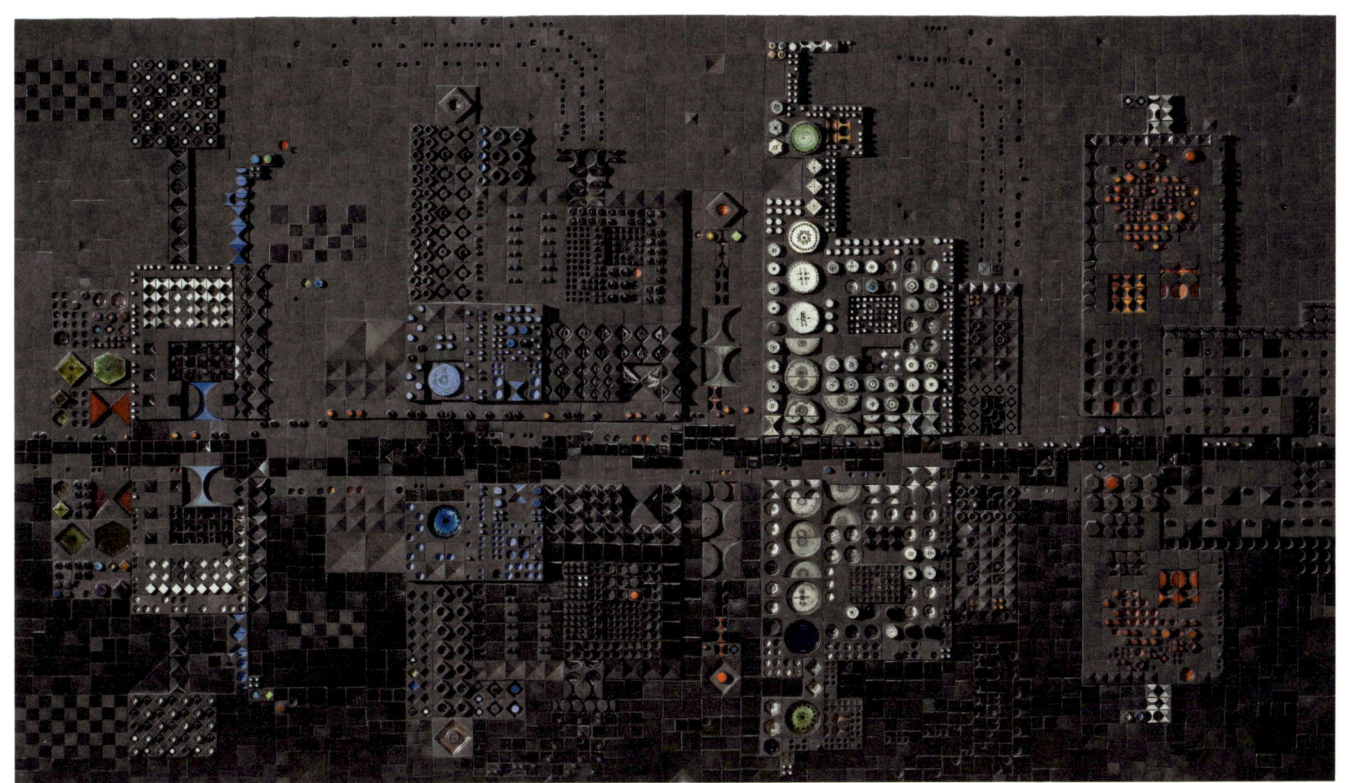

From medieval times, Finnish men have owned and used a knife called a puukko. Both weapon and all-purpose tool, a puukko was used for hunting, fishing, soldiering, preparing food, eating, handicrafts and more. Women had their own version, an indispensable domestic and kitchen tool. Traditionally, a puukko was carried in a leather sheath on the belt, although the practice was banned in 1972. However, puukkos are still dusted off for ceremonial occasions and often given as gifts. The most prized are still made by hand.

The puukko is a fitting emblem of Finnish culture: utilitarian, multi-functional, ergonomic and well-designed. It is a tool for survival, conjuring up images of the hardy and resilient Finns. An object owned by many in Finland, regardless of privilege or position, it is a link to a shared history. Venerated for all of these things, the puukko's uncompromising usefulness, enduring symbolism and simple beauty is a great insight into the Finnish approach to everyday objects.

TOOLS FOR LIVING
PUUKKO

Previous and this page
Matti Heiskanen is a traditional Finnish knife-maker: a 'puukkomestari'. The puukko has a short blade with a flat back, allowing the user to put pressure on the blade with their thumb, and a leather sheath which can be attached to a belt.

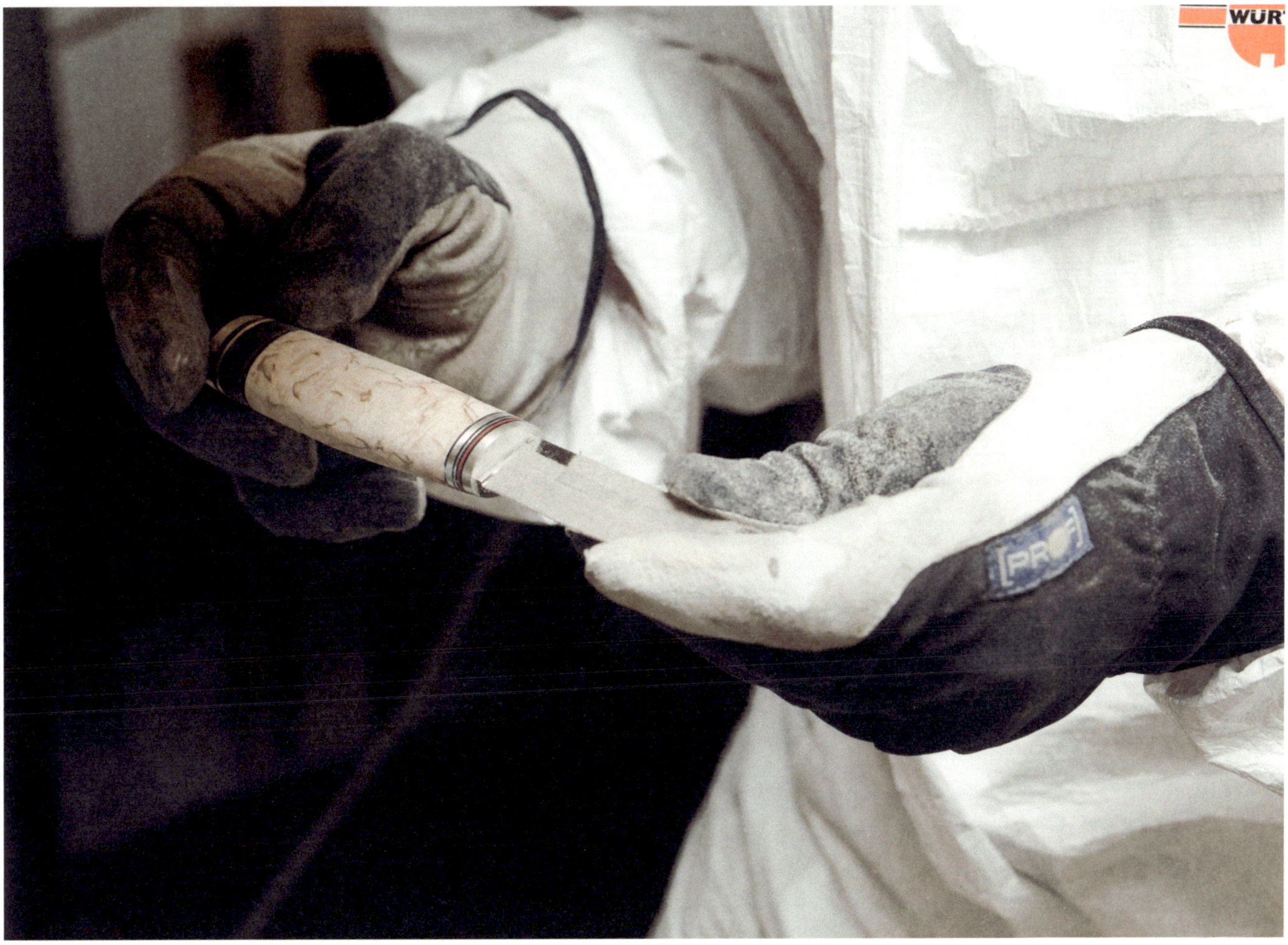

SKILLS AND TRADITIONS

In 2009, designer Simo Heikkilä invited a group of international designers to engage in a dying craft and a symbol of Finnish culture by reworking the Sami knife, or leuku. The leuku is a larger version of a puukko and is used for all kinds of practical tasks, such as butchering and wood cutting.

In all, 22 designers, including Ronan and Erwan Bouroullec, Konstantin Grcic and Jasper Morrison, took part in the project, expanding the knife's function, reinterpreting its traditional form and generally exploring how this staple tool could be bettered.

'The reason I undertook this project is simple,' says Heikkilä. 'Every culture has its own cultural objects, but many, many skills are vanishing as the world globalises. It's causing a dramatic change in everyday objects: plastics are being used instead of woods, and so on. I knew some Sami master craftspeople, although the last one has died now. The whole project was built around his skill.'

Each designer received an original knife made by the Sami craftsman and was given the simple brief to make it better. 'All prototypes had to be made in Finland,' says Heikkilä. 'That was important. So the skills of the knife-makers we have here were used fully.'

Heikkilä particularly singles out Konstantin Grcic's design. 'It was especially good,' he says. 'He redesigned the knife's handle so it was easier to grasp with gloves on. Of course, it is very cold where these knives are used…'

For his own contemporary interpretation of a leuku, Heikkilä created a handle in plywood and dyed it red, making it easier to find if dropped in the natural environment. He also repaired an old leather sheath by covering it in heat-shrunk PVC.

Designer, teacher, collaborator, Simo Heikkilä is a guardian of Finnish design. With his concern over dying craft skills, his preservation of drawing skills and his network of skilled workmen, he has an eye on the bigger picture.

Heikkilä lives and works in the countryside near Jyväskylä. His work is increasingly informed by the local crafts and skills that surround him. And it is increasingly celebrated too: he won the Pro Finlandia medal in 2003 and the prestigious Kaj Franck design prize in 2011.

PENCIL-AIDED DESIGN
SIMO HEIKKILÄ

Somehow my philosophies are very simple: everything has to be done to scale.

SIMO HEIKKILÄ

Previous page
This image was taken at Fiskars, where Heikkilä used to live and work. He now lives near Jyväskylä in a purpose-built building that is home, studio and gallery.

Above
The Iron Divan 2000 is an exercise in human ergonomics.

A sketch for the Rattan Lounge Chair 1999 shows Simo Heikkilä's pencil-aided design.

You won the Kaj Franck award recently. What did that mean to you?
It meant a lot. As I have become older, my thoughts and ideas have become somehow more strict and I am quite critical about what is happening around me.

Critical of the design scene in general or critical of your own work?
I have an idea of how the world could be. There is so much nonsense around us. It is, of course, not my duty to police design, but I have tried to do my best here in Finland anyway. Of course, the younger generation must also have the opportunity to create and be creative and follow their own lines and so on. But what is the price then? We can evaluate it. For example, in China there are at least 8,000 new design students every spring and everybody wants to design something. So it's a dilemma.

Is there a solution?
Yes, it's coming. But there are problems in countries like China where the rapid change of the life from rural to urban is destroying everything which is valuable. The very simple fine things, the cooking traditions, are nothing any more, and so on. And this happens without any critics.

In Finland, too, there was a move from rural to urban that happened quickly.
Yes, it was quite quick. And in Japan it was the same. So some people have said that that's the reason why Japanese and Finnish designers have a certain kind of relationship.

Do you think that there is some kind of parallel?
What I have noticed during my trips there is what we call farmer life: those objects created in Japan and those we have in Finland look very, very similar and they have the same function. Of course, part of the reason for that is that we have maybe used wood in the same way, except for bamboo. The mentality is similar: it has been very easy to become friends with Japanese designers. I have been in Japan 27 times since 1981, visiting almost yearly. This collegial network is very important. And this project for the Sami knife, getting these designers together, was based on this network.

Tell me about teaching at Aalto University: how long have you been doing that?
I have been doing this a long time, but as a designer, maybe for 20 years. Somehow my philosophies are very simple: everything has to be done to scale. I don't trust CAD pictures and such things. You only learn through prototyping and contact with the object.

How do you work?
I draw by hand, and I call it PAD: pencil-aided design! Forget the computer and sketch—and make as many beautiful drawings as possible. Beauty is very important in my teaching. We are an art school. The words art and beauty must be included, automatically, more or less.

When did your design career begin? Did you study design?
Yes. I graduated in 1967. But at first I practised interior design. I was independent, working in my own one-man office, and I designed shops and exhibitions for Marimekko. So it was a start. Then I realized that maybe I had something to say about things and I began designing furniture. First I decided to do furniture in solid birch. I called a master model-maker, Kari Virtanen, and we went for two weeks to Lapland and made models. This is how it started, and somehow I continued.

What inspires you now?
I was in Italy one summer and during that trip I found something… But I cannot analyse it even now. I understood that I had to do something that is useful; something that has nice proportions, beauty, and that is quite natural. The designers I have followed are few. The most important has been Maarten Van Severen. He had the talent, but also he was master at constructive thinking and so on. Construction is so important to me. That comes first, then beauty and then the rest.

You have produced some collections with green wood too…
This kind of thinking comes from the local masters. The material is the framework for everything.

Is it satisfying to work with those kind of crafts?
Of course. This is another kind of network.

There are some beautiful ergonomic shapes in your work.
Yes! Ergonomics are so important. First comes the ergonomics, then comes the construction and then comes the visual.

Is there anything in your work that you would say is specifically Finnish?
The reason why I'm working and staying here in Finland is, of course, the four seasons of the year: they are very clear. There are not many thoughts behind it. It is just my landscape. One word I forgot to mention about my work: humour. A very dry humour!

> **I realised that maybe I had something to say about things.**
>
> SIMO HEIKKILÄ

This page
Simplicity, says Heikkilä, is a very Finnish trait. He adds that simple, beautiful objects are universally understood. Local production is integral to many of his designs, such as these Wooden Bowls 2003–2006.

Top left
The Sauna Stool 1998 is made from aspen and birch bark.

Bottom left
An honest, elegant use of plywood was behind the design of the Visa Chair 1991.

Harri Koskinen still gets excited when he visits factories. The thrill, he says, is in finding ways to maximise the capabilities of the industrial machinery at his disposal. Armi Ratia once described Marimekko dresses blowing in the breeze outside an American store as 'like Finnish flags', the bright printed fabrics as recognisable as the Blue Cross. And Alvar Aalto famously championed a manufacturing industry that could benefit society.

Design and industry have a special relationship in Finland. Social agendas and commercial ambitions have long been entwined. Mass-produced and mass-admired, Finnish design is an important export. But arguably it is the wide distribution of Finnish ideals and values, packaged among the drinking glasses, crockery, phones and fashion, that has the greater influence, both at home and abroad.

DESIGNER AND INDUSTRY

You would not get far in a discussion about contemporary Finnish design before Harri Koskinen's name came up. He has become the recognisable face of new Finnish design. His main preoccupations—everyday design, innovation in products and manufacturing, refreshing and renewing traditions, all tackled without pretence or ego—are those of the wider industry.

His Block Lamp, designed when a student, attracted so much interest that he set up his own studio, Friends of Industry, after graduating from the former University of Art and Design Helsinki. It has since produced everything from smoke alarms to artworks to kitchens. He has now his own brand, Harri Koskinen Works, and his appointment as design director at Iittala confirms his influential position in Finland's design firmament.

TOEING THE TECHNICAL LINE
HARRI KOSKINEN

Were you full of ideas as a child?
I was brought up in the middle of a forest with no neighbours in sight. I used to build tracks for my play cars, which I found fascinating. In my mind I'd scale myself down to the size of the cars and my imagination would soar.

What do you regard as the most inspiring stage of the design process?
Factory visits are really interesting. It's inspiring to see and experience something new as well as to consider one's part in that world. When producing things for mass production, you need to consider the play of values throughout the process: from the designer's table or even thoughts, then to the engineers and on to all the commercial people involved. When you are drawing the mould you might be playing with nanometres. Then there is the final product, made by a machine: will it be good enough for the end users? It's like a great game.

Where does your fondness and understanding of industry stem from?
It has to stem from the Iittala glass factory where I first worked. Machinery, equipment and a romantic industrial notion are the best inspiration. All designers should be required to work at a factory during their studies. During that time I was working on projects all the time where I was exploring what is possible and what is not. And of course it was a constant quest to explore how to really stretch these boundaries.

That relationship is so strong that you named your studio after it…
Yes. I started Friends of Industry in 2000, and of course it's like a kind of philosophy. How I see it is that I need to have a good relationship with the clients I am working with, so I am acting as a friend would. I've always been fascinated by factories. I think it's about the contrast with where I'm from, the countryside. So that is perhaps why I found it interesting initially.

But then, during my education as an industrial designer, I began to really appreciate the work of engineers. It's that simple. Also, when I look at things that need to be produced in an efficient way, this stimulates my thinking. I enjoy the way that machines are put under human control and how all the mistakes are ironed out. Of course mistakes do happen all the time in the production process and there are many things to work on…

Does that relationship with the natural world you grew up in play an important role in your designs?
I've consciously tried to avoid nature-inspired themes. Being inspired by nature was an integral part of myth construction about Finland during the 1950s and 1960s. But many areas in my personal life are connected to nature. I enjoy hunting, picking berries and mushrooms, trekking and cross-country skiing.

Perhaps your work reflects a different Finnish culture: the industrially minded one? You have designed such a variety of work. Which do you think are the most important?
One highlight is the Block Lamp. I designed it as part of my student studies and then Design House Stockholm wanted to produce it. But from my perspective there are also things that are not so well known.

When I was first employed by Iittala in 1998 I was commissioned to make a centrepiece and a lantern for the Art Works glassware collection. Then I was invited to work with Hackman where I made a barbeque set and in parallel I was invited by Arabia to make some ceramic containers. So that was really great as a young designer right out of school. And then I began working for Issey Miyake.

All of that work was a sort of staircase for me. But no designer would like to point out the classics of their career. They would prefer to talk about future things; what is happening next year.

> **Machinery, equipment and a romantic industrial notion are the best inspiration. All designers should be required to work at a factory during their studies.**
>
> HARRI KOSKINEN

Koskinen designed the Block Lamp in 1996 as a student project and it is now considered something of a contemporary classic. The rendition of glass as an icy block is in the tradition of other great Finnish designers such as Tapio Wirkkala.

The Lento lounge chair 2012 for Artek.

A prototype design for the Valoisa light 2012 for Marimekko.

And what is happening next?
I have developed a backpack for Paratroopers with an aluminium frame. The manufacturer produced the same frame for three decades without any changes. It had 40 welding points; we reduced it to only four just by bending the aluminium. It has to withstand stress, being dropped, and so on. It's a fascinating ergonomic study.

What would be a dream product to design?
A bicycle. It would be quite a challenge.

When are you satisfied with your designs?
I'm never completely satisfied. But if I had to mention something, I'd say I'm particularly satisfied with the smoke alarm I designed for Jalo Helsinki. That has aroused a great deal of fascination and acclaim.

Do you consciously strive to develop your creative side?
Yes. I travel quite a lot, although on leisure only in Finland. I always keep my notebook and camera with me when I'm travelling abroad.

Are you more of an artist or engineer?
Unfortunately I'm mostly a secretary, judging by the amount of time I spend on e-mails and maintaining contacts. Otherwise I mainly think on a technical line. Free expression with a purely aesthetic purpose is somehow difficult for me.

The work of a designer is becoming increasingly abstract. Is that true of your work?
At least half of the projects carried out by my studio are of a non-material nature. Of course it's only the concrete projects that people see. I enjoy finding structural solutions and thinking about usability within product design. Different sensor technologies, for example, are fascinating.

With your own studio, you've produced everything from trucks to metalwork to glass. Is there any particular material or process that you most enjoy?
I have decided to rent a wood workshop and so I think now I'm going to spend more time there with those materials. Building things by myself is really rewarding.

Is that a problem with getting too successful? That you don't get so much hands-on time?
Yes. Most of my time is spent communicating with clients. But I still feel like I am a creator rather than a spokesperson for the business. I am really happy to realise that and now that I have the workshop I feel it's going to be like a new beginning—hopefully.

And what about your role at Iittala? Was that something you hoped for? You have a long history with the brand.
It is sort of dream work for me; that I can have this role outside my studio activities where I learn so much about procedures, meet many new people and get to work with these processes. So I have nothing to complain about.

What about being Finnish? Is that something you reflect upon?
It's something I don't seek either to emphasise or avoid. I am fortunate and happy to be Finnish.

Right
Glass has proven to have enduring appeal for Harri Koskinen. Just like Kaj Franck before him, he produces experimental studio glass in limited editions, free of the constraints of the production line. The Kohta carafe, the Jalusta stand and the Pokaali goblet are all part of Iittalla's Art Works collection 2009.

Below
Koskinen's collaboration with Iittala began at university, when he won a scholarship to spend three months at its glassworks factory. He became an in-house designer on graduation, created its first Art Works collection in 2009 and is now design director of the brand.

> I've consciously tried to avoid nature-inspired themes. Being inspired by nature was an integral part of myth construction about Finland during the 1950s and 1960s.
>
> **HARRI KOSKINEN**

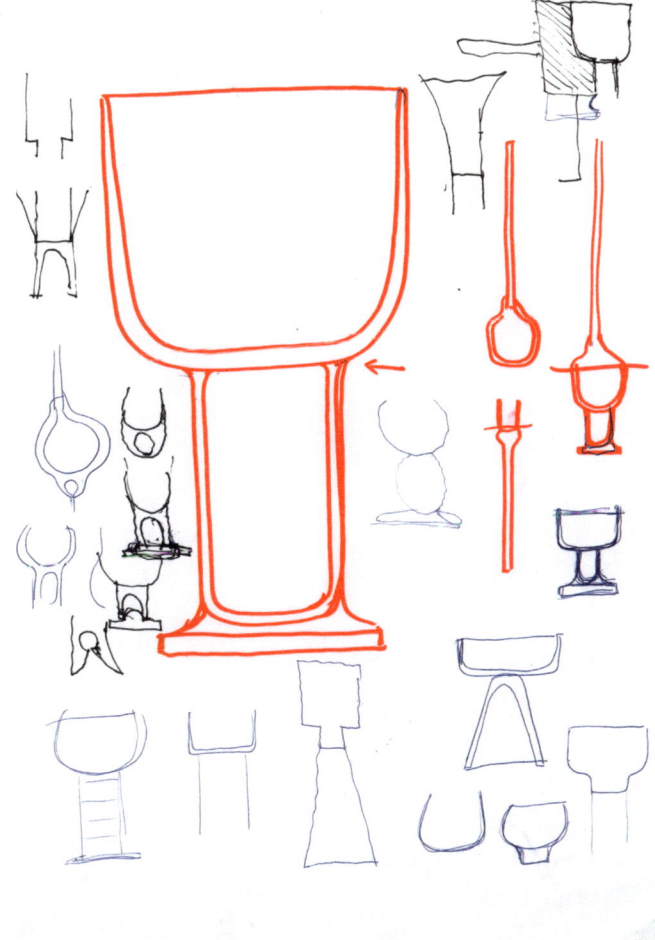

This page
Iittala's successful Oma collection of flexible, simple, functional tableware preceded Koskinen's appointment as design director.

Right
The Kupu smoke alarm for Jalo Helsinki demonstrates Koskinen beautifying an everyday object. It is simple, affordable, and easy to use and install.

> I'm never completely satisfied. But if I had to pick something, I'd say the smoke alarm I designed for Jalo Helsinki.
>
> HARRI KOSKINEN

With his playful forms and bright colours, Eero Aarnio's work is an exception from that of many other Finnish designers. He is perhaps best known for his experimental chairs and ground-breaking use of plastic: his Ball Chair has appeared in a Bond movie and on the cover of Playboy magazine. In recent years, he has designed products for Magis and Serralunga.

Aarnio lives and works in Veikkola, southern Finland, in a studio he designed for himself. He opted for white interiors as a clean backdrop for his famous love of colour. The space evolves along with the seasons, while the prototypes of whatever he is working on at the time bring their own vivid array of hues too.

STANDING APART
EERO AARNIO

You stand out from other Finnish designers through your use of colour and playful designs. Where does your individual style stem from?
Everyone has their own signature. I've always had my own way of thinking and I don't want to repeat what's been done before.

Your animal forms, for instance, are sweet yet rather simplistic. How do you balance these qualities?
Creating these types of products is based on a solid background in furniture design for public spaces. It requires an understanding of ergonomics and dimensions, as well as a positive attitude towards industrial design to ensure reasonable pricing.

What is the secret behind timelessness?
No such thing exists. Someone recently asked what I wished I'd invented and my answer was 'a wheel'! Objects like a spoon, safety pin or pen are always functional and people don't necessarily even think along the lines of who designed them.

What is your design ideology?
If I create an object I'm happy with, I know others will be too. Whether or not I wish to look at it is the criterion. If the creative process keeps getting stuck, it won't work. A sign of a good idea is that the productive stages progress quickly. A good idea is like an aphorism.

What motivates you?
When I create a product, I immediately think of another one. I can't quite help it. Even now I have a whole line of good ideas waiting. Manufacture is the bottleneck. I'm curious, inventive and fast. During the Second World War, when Helsinki was being bombed, we slept with our shoes on ready to run. I was always the first down in the bomb shelter even though we lived on the top floor.

The Ball Chair was a particularly important design for you, how did it happen?
We had just moved to a Helsinki suburb. We had no furniture, not even a lamp in the kitchen. It was there that I decided to draw a very big chair, which could seat the whole family. I had just visited a Turku boatyard and had seen a fibreglass boat for the first time in my life. I thought about how the material could achieve all forms.

Material plays a key role in your work. What qualities are you looking for?
The potential of each material has always been my starting point. The Ball Chair couldn't be made from wood. Or perhaps it could, but it would make no sense. I'm currently working on an invisible glass chair. And this is one of my wackiest ideas: sewing a pair of magnetic metal trousers and installing the opposite magnetic field in the floor, so you can sit in the air. I'm intrigued by the thought of creating something that stops people in their tracks. I created the Ball Chair after becoming a freelancer. The idea worked then and it continues to work now.

Any new techniques that have inspired you recently?
I've been commissioning small objects as 3D models. Those who hold the purse strings—i.e., the CEOs—often have no clue when it comes to drawings. But when they see a model, they say: 'Oh, this is nice.' We then decide on a suitable mould.

Do you dream of designing something in particular?
I'd like to design a car. No-one has thought to ask me yet. I already know what kind of car I'd create: a yummy, modern-looking one.

Do you get a lot of requests?
I do from abroad. Magis and Serralunga from Italy contacted me recently. In Finland I approach manufacturers myself. When I get an idea, I think about a suitable producer and get in contact.

Do you follow the younger generations work?
I do not follow it in that way, but as a designer I'm like a vacuum cleaner. I absorb everything that comes in front of me. You never know what you might need. Architects inspire me: Frank Gehry is one of my idols. I visited the Guggenheim in Bilbao, as soon as it was completed, and I also visited the Corbusier church at Ronchamp. In America I drove 800 miles to see Frank Lloyd Wright's Fallingwater. I also stayed in the Imperial Hotel in Tokyo before it was torn down. I am also interested in Richard Meier and IM Pei. And Zaha Hadid is just awesome. I am really disappointed the Guggenheim Museum did not come to Helsinki.

What do you think will change material-oriented design?
Recyclability will be key: all this material simply cannot stay here and clog up the planet. If only our oceans could be cleared of the waste.

Do you plan to keep on designing?
What else would I do? This is fun. Work has never felt like work. And if it has, it's because I've had a bad idea. Who knows what I'll still get to do?

Right and following pages
Aarnio's studio is as characterful and playful as the man himself. Amongst his work are several iconic forms and many humorous designs such as the Puppy for Magis.

> **A sign of a good idea is that the productive stages progress quickly. A good idea is like an aphorism.**
>
> EERO AARNIO

Pastil Chair 1968.

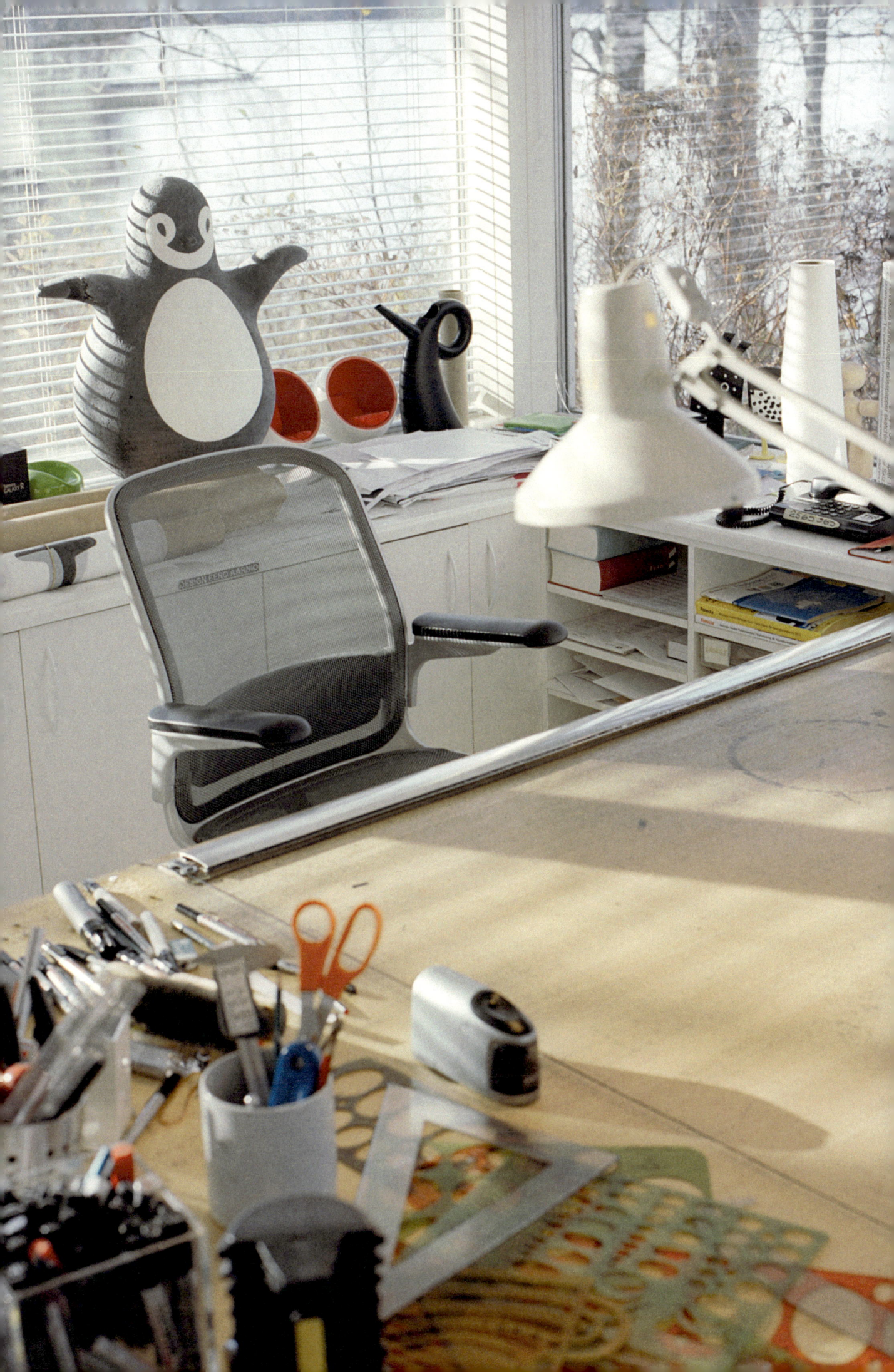

The Bubble Chair 1968 is a piece of furniture that epitomises the swinging 1960s. It is also a great example of Aarnio's highly confident design style.

> **The potential of each material has always been my starting point. The Ball Chair couldn't be made from wood. Or perhaps it could, but it would make no sense.**
>
> EERO AARNIO

Who would have thought that a small company producing oilcloth would become internationally synonymous with Finnish design? Perhaps Armi Ratia, the strong-willed founder of Marimekko who in 1951 fused her commercial sensibility with a desire to bring colour, life and energy into the homes of a depressed nation.

Today, Marimekko is a pattern powerhouse with real global reach, making furnishing fabric, tableware, clothing, bags and more. And yet it remains very much an idealistic, domestic brand, just as it was in the beginning. Minna Kemell-Kutvonen, Marimekko's creative director, explains how the simple but compelling values of this quintessentially Finnish brand endure.

EVERYDAY AESTHETICS
MARIMEKKO

Armi Ratia founded Marimekko in 1951, not long after the war had ended. Was it an optimistic time?
Optimistic, yes. But all in all, Finland was really grey at that time. We really live by nature, and maybe that is also the reason why we are so practical. Armi was a very strong woman and her husband owned an oilcloth company. Together they tried to find how to use the fabric. They needed some creative energy, and Armi was a creative woman. They started to print a cotton fabric and then Armi founded Marimekko.

Were the printed fabrics a success from the start?
Because the fabrics were so strong and so colourful and because most Finnish homes were really small, people didn't know how to use them. Then Armi decided they would do some clothing and dresses. This first fashion show happened in 1951 and was really strong. After that, Marimekko became better known and people started to discover our other products and to use them in the home.

Was the use of bright and vibrant colour always important?
Yes. Colour was always something really special. It was not exactly the use of strong and proud colours on their own, but something about their combinations that was interesting. Back then, the designers found that, of course, we didn't have so many colours. They had to mix them to make something new. One of Armi's slogans was: 'We are so rich, we have empty hands.' You have to use all of your creativity when you don't have so many things.

Why was Armi so driven?
Armi and all the designers, the other creative people who were working with her, really wanted to bring a kind of happiness to people's everyday lives.

The idea that products should be really useful and easy to use in every area of life, is that just as important today?
Yes. I think people in Finland are basically practical. You can see that in our functionalism and aesthetic. I think that Marimekko's design philosophy is about making something practical that can also be an aesthetic for everyday life.

Finland's position is interesting too. We're in the middle of two different cultures, East and West. When we talk about aesthetic understanding and culture, this is important. I think there is a really interesting culture that we've gained from the East: more romantic, ornamental and so on. A rich aesthetic. Then from the West and Scandinavia comes a minimalistic and graphical tradition and so on. In Finland, we have a lovely way of mixing them together.

What about the success of the company? And its longevity? Is there any secret to it?
I think it's that we trust the future. Whether the times are hard or good or whatever it is, we trust the future. Also we trust people: our designers and their creativity. But then, of course, you have to be a little bit lucky too. Quite often I hear that Marimekko is about strong colours and graphical shapes and so on, but that is only one side. We have many different languages: they are all really pure and based on a designer's thinking. I believe that because our design palette is quite wide, and can be different things at different times, they are…

They appeal to different people?
Yes. We don't close all the doors. As a business model, there is much to admire: your product is very flexible, adaptable and has universal appeal. If you think about our Uniko pattern and even our stripes, there is some strong message there. You might even consider the stripes to have a democratic message. Also those are really important things; there is something there that is more than only a product. There is some kind of social thinking.

There are a lot of strong women behind the brand—such as Armi Ratia, Maija Isola and Vuokko Nurmesniemi—and in Finnish design in general. Is there something particular about Finnish culture that encourages women?
In Finland our society is quite democratic. The reason for this, I think, is that there have always been so many things to do. If you think about a rural family, for example, women have to do a lot in order to manage their everyday life. And in all those wars, women had to manage their family because their husband was in the war. We are quite new to the city. And also our men are so open-minded!

What makes a great Marimekko print?
I think there is only trust or intuition. That is the only way.

> I think there is a really interesting culture that we've gained from the East: more romantic, ornamental and so on. A rich aesthetic.
>
> MINNA KEMELL-KUTVONEN

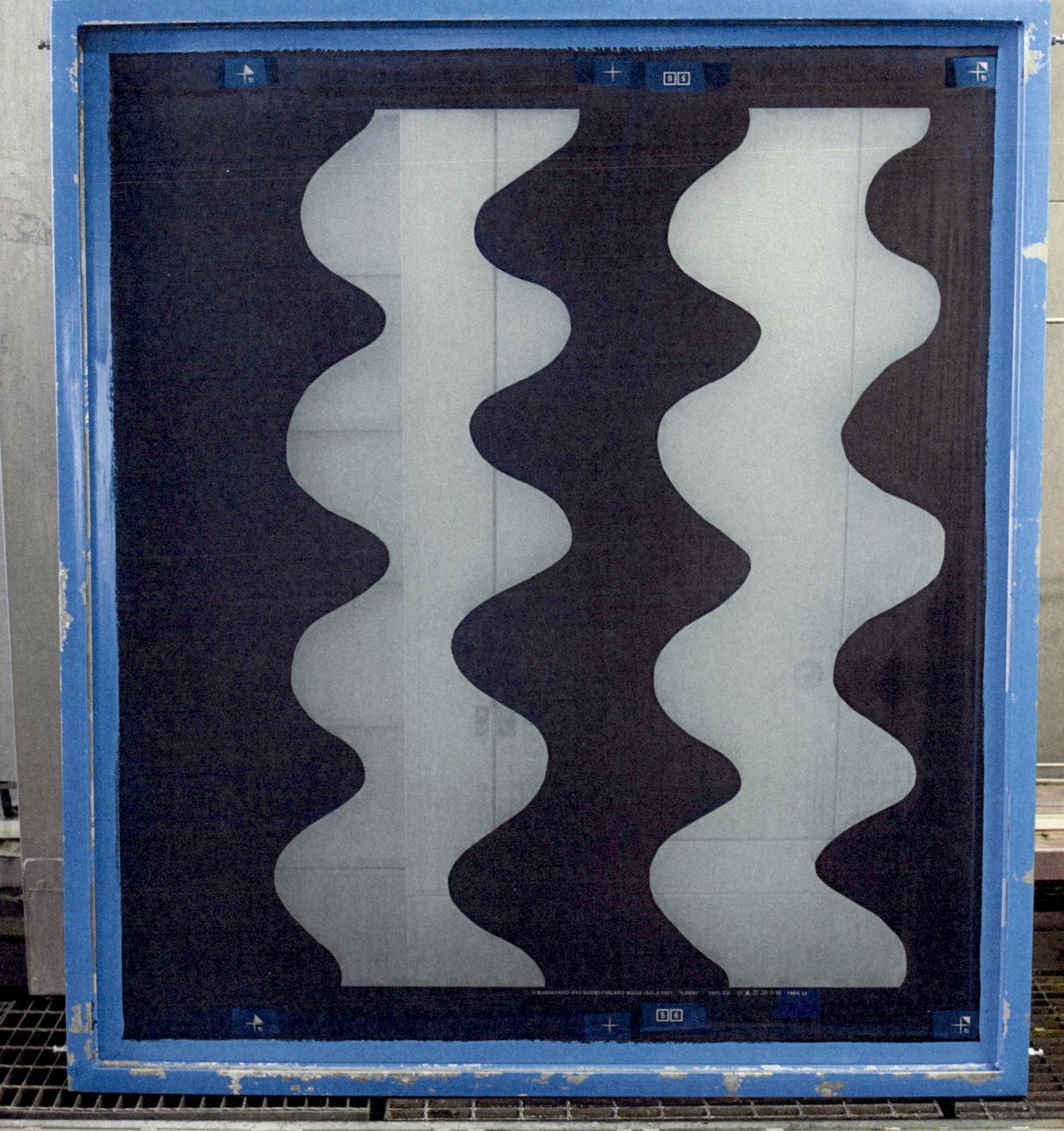

Previous page
The Jurmo fabric, by Aino-Maija Metsola, was inspired by the rocky landscape of Jurmo island in Western Finland.

Left
Minna Kemell-Kutvonen.

This page
A used screen showing the Seagull pattern by Maija Isola.

The pinboard in the Marimekko fashion design studio is a riot of patterns. Marimekko fashion launched in 1951 with a show at the Kalastajatorppa Hotel and really took off after Jackie Kennedy bought several dresses in 1960.

Colour was always special. It was not exactly the use of strong and proud colours on their own, but something about their combinations.

MINNA KEMELL-KUTVONEN

Nature is an important thing for us in both Finland and Japan. So that is a common point; my starting point.

SAWAKO URA

Above
Sawako Ura is the latest talented Japanese designer to work with Marimekko, following in the footsteps of Katsuji Wakisaka and Fujiwo Ishimoto. Ishimoto is Ura's mentor and inspiration. His influence can be seen in the colour palette and style of designs such as Tunturipöllö (Snowy Owl).

Right
Aino Maija Metsola, pictured wearing her own design, is behind some of Marimekko's most significant new designs. She describes her working methods as 'free'. She sketches by hand and favours felt tips for colour.

I sketch by hand and then scan the drawings into the computer. Sometimes there is a lot of work to do, but other times it is already there.

AINO MAIJA METSOLA

The Marimekko factory produces 1.2 million metres of fabric every year. Although partly automated, the process remains remarkably similar to the days when workers gathered around a table with screens. The amount of ink applied is measured by an experienced hand while each bolt of fabric is laboriously checked by an expert eye.

Armi Ratia founded Marimekko in 1951. It was an interesting time because the war had finished and we could look towards some kind of future.

MINNA KEMELL-KUTVONEN

Kuuskajaskari 2012
by Aino-Maija Metsola.

Siirtolapuutarha (Allotment) 2010 by Maija Louekari.

Tiikeri (Tiger) 2012
by Sawako Ura.

Green Green 1975
by Katsuji Wakisaka.

Aatto (Eve) 1989
by Fujiwo Ishimoto.

Siren 1964
by Armi Ratia.

Ginkgo 2008
by Kristina Isola.

Lokki (Seagull) 1961
by Maija Isola.

Istuva Härkä (Sitting Bull) 1967
by Maija Isola.

Ukkospilvi (Thundercloud) 1980
by Fujiwo Ishimoto.

Vattenblänk (Glittering Water) 2011 by Astrid Sylwan.

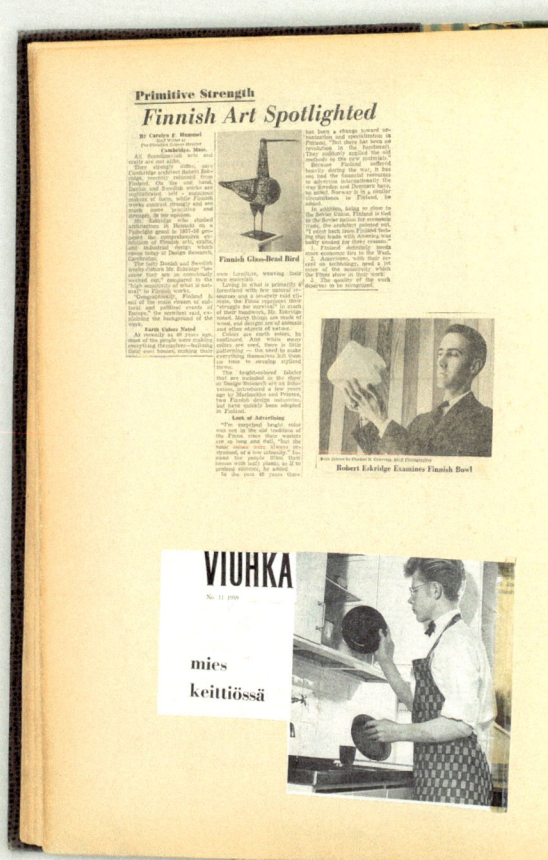

Marimekko's archive lies a stone's throw from where high-tech printing machines generate reams of new fabric. In here are samples and swatches of the 3,500 prints and myriad colourways it has produced since 1951. Carefully pasted press cuttings in fabric-bound journals reveal a miraculous journey as this small company grew into an international sensation.

But perhaps what is most revealing about the contents of these dusty journals and catalogues is the remarkable consistency of the Marimekko message, which transcends the changing fashions. From start to finish, on page after page, the warm and joyful imagery, and energetic, exciting prints sing an infectious and brilliantly uplifting song.

A HISTORY REMEMBERED
MARIMEKKO INVENTORY

Top
In 1951, press attention was still a novelty. The careful and playful way articles were pasted is telling of the youth of the new company.

Bottom
In 1965, Marimekko was at its height, both at home and abroad, and was making all sorts of goods, sunglasses for children included.

DESIGNER AND INDUSTRY

Top
In 1966, Life magazine ran an extensive feature on Marimekko, juxtaposing bright, light fashion with classic Finnish scenery.

Bottom
In the late 1970s, Marimekko homeware was a popular feature in interior magazines, as in this bold tableau of yellow carpets and green Unikko.

Top
Linjaviitta dress 1967
by Annika Rimala
Galleria pattern 1954
by Vuokko Nurmesniemi.

Bottom
Dress in Pitsihuvila pattern 1958
by Vuokko Nurmesniemi.

Top right
Raincoat 1957
by Vuokko Nurmesniemi.

Bottom right
Kivijalkamekko dress 1957
Pattern Piccolo 1953
by Vuokko Nurmesniemi.

DESIGNER AND INDUSTRY

Top
Dress from the late 1950s by Vuokko Nurmesniemi.

Bottom
Pitsihuvila dress 1951 by Riitta ImmonenCaramba pattern by Elis Muona.

Top right
Nightgowns, Tasaraita collection 1968 by Annika Rimala.

Bottom right
Santa Margareta dress, 1960 Pattern Paituli by Vuokko Nurmesniemi.

MARIMEKKO INVENTORY

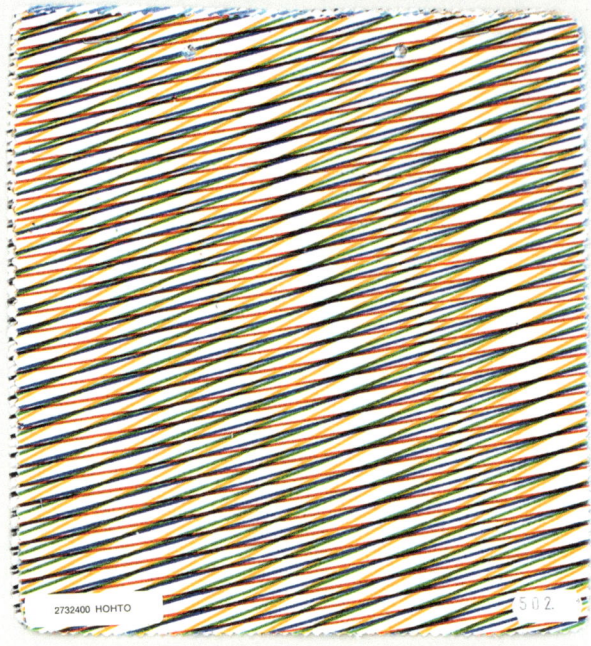
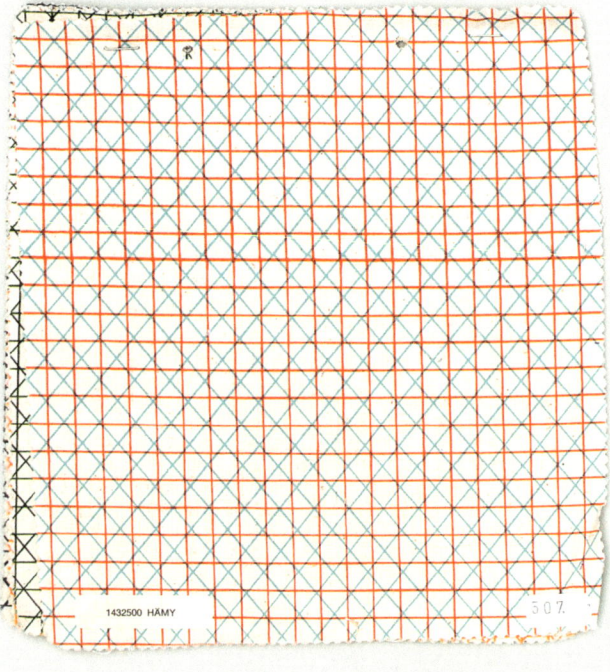

Kaste, Hohto, Hämy and Pouta 1981 swatches, from the more than 300 designs created for Marimekko by Fujiwo Ishimoto.

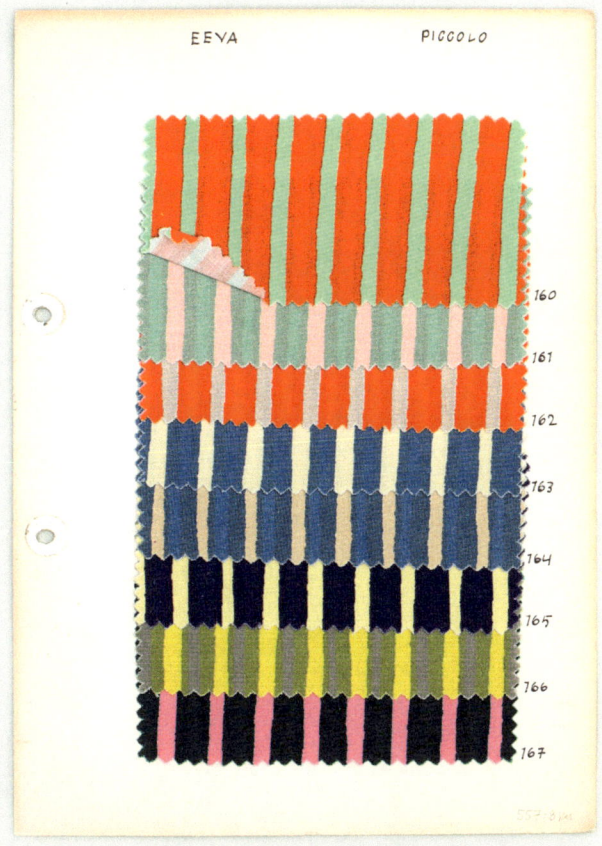
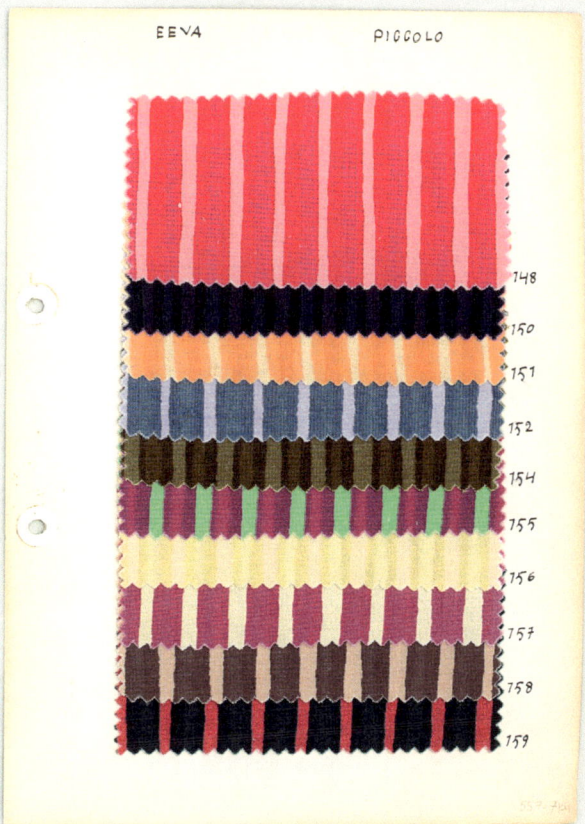

Colour swatch testing cards for Piccolo 1953 and Lumimarja 2005 reveal the multitude of colour combinations tried for each print.

Yrjö Kukkapuro is a Finnish designer whose iconic pieces, including the Karuselli and Ateljee chairs and the Saturnus series, are well known for being brave and innovative: the curvaceous shells, skeletal forms and bold colours of his work have always stood apart. But Kukkapuro's work isn't theatrical or superficial. His starting points are ergonomics and function and his designs are constantly evolving to improve both.

He works at his Atelier Kukkapuro in Kauniainen, built in 1968, which he shares with his wife, the graphic artist Irmeli Kukkapuro. He is the creative director of Avarte and his work has been exhibited at the MoMA, the V&A and the Vitra Design Museum. Recently, Kukkapuro's famous Karuselli chair has been relaunched by Artek.

EVOLUTION AND REVOLUTION
YRJÖ KUKKAPURO

When did you first get involved with industrial design?
I have always been into arts and I was going to be an artist. My intention was to study graphics, but a friend of mine convinced me to work at a furniture factory and I ended up studying interior arts, which then consisted of product and interior design, materials and everything. At that time design was a non-existent word in Finland.

I graduated just after the war when designers were in demand because the construction business was booming. I have never regretted moving into product and interiors, though, because I have enjoyed this profession very much. From the very beginning I managed to design products that were selected for exhibitions. The profession felt very natural to me. I guess this became my calling.

What are your habits when it comes to the design process?
The design process almost always starts with architecture. Architecture is the mother of all arts! In 1957 I heard a lecture about ergonomics in Finland by Dr Bengt Åkerblom from Sweden. That changed everything. Just like that I realised that I had to design reflections of the human body.

I started working on all sorts of materials to create a shell for the body and worked on my sculptures for many years. I didn't do one single drawing! In 1965 the Karuselli chair was ready for production. I didn't do any drawings until the 1970s when we moved into industrial production and needed them. When post-modernism arrived I was ready for it because I was tired of functionalism. That's when I really started sketching and using colour. Ergonomics are still important and everybody knows this, everybody. I have seen a chair made in Egypt 3,200 years ago and it's almost the same as my bamboo chair.

What helps your creativity?
I like working in my atelier because I've been there for 45 years. I can learn from my past mistakes. The form comes when the technical aspects, the structure and ergonomics are right. When there is clarity, the aesthetics come naturally.

What compels you to create?
I get excited when I get interesting requests from people. It can be a concert hall, a restaurant or an office. Right now I'm excited about local production. These days sustainability is a must. We are fighting very much to keep production here. My newest chairs are all wood and made in a nearby village.

Also functions are very, very important for me: the different needs of architecture, or needs of the houses where the furniture will be, whether they be homes or other buildings.

And are you always working on something new?
For the last 40 years I have been developing my chairs, bettering them all the time. It's hard to say if they're new.

Do you consider yourself part of a Finnish design tradition?
My grandfather made his own house, the table and even the spoons. A hundred years ago we were self-sufficient and I think that has had an effect on my design, which is very simple, functional and based on needs. I tried to design according to international aesthetics, so that my work could be accepted around the world. I didn't think I was particularly Finnish; I used materials from all over the world.

Now lately I have had this thought that perhaps my designs do have some Finnishness that reflects my native country, its nature and my ancestors' work. I am coming from old traditions and it's maybe that; this Finnish simplicity and this idea of the self-made. But then there are also influences around from America and Italy and everywhere—all around. I feel more international.

Where can we see that influence in your work?
Well, it's really funny because I have been following this simplifying theme all the time. But then I saw my work from the 1980s, when we made very, very, very post-modern things, and I saw the influences of maybe Russia or somewhere in some of the details. The forms are coming across. But it was subconscious. And they [the traditional details] are so nice, they are the best in the world; I could cry they are so nice.

Details are important in your designs. Do you design the fittings and fixtures for your designs too?
They are very important; the connectors. It gives some richness to the chair. I worked many months on one connection. I simplified it and now it works very well.

And a simple colour palette too?
Basic colours; many basic colours. I think they are best for me.

If you had to sum up what the Finnish creative philosophy is, what would you say?
I think that Finnish design means very high quality aesthetics, ergonomics and function. We are good at specialising in glass, furniture and textiles. That's how we maintain our reputation.

Kukkapuro, too, made his own house and most of the things in it. The wing-like roof of his studio is made of concrete, which was particularly difficult to achieve in 1968 when it was built.

My grandfather made his own house, the table and even the spoons.

YRJÖ KUKKAPURO

Untitled 2012
by Irmeli Kukkapuro.

> **Basic colours; many basic colours. I think they are best for me.**
> YRJÖ KUKKAPURO

The Sirkus chair is destined for forward-thinking offices. Its seat is made from a pressed birch plywood shell.

**A hundred years ago we were
self-sufficient and I think
that has had an affect on
my designing, which is very simple,
functional and based on needs.**

YRJÖ KUKKAPURO

Graphic lines, an irrepressible ergonomic curve and an architectural construction characterise Kukkapuro's careful and considerate work. His Karuselli chair 1964, is one of the most celebrated chair designs ever produced.

By the 1950s, Vuokko Nurmesniemi had already invented the bold graphic prints that were to revolutionise Finnish print design. By the 1960s, she had moved on to creating the daring, sculptural and liberating dresses that caught the attention of the world. By the 1980s, she had abandoned man-made fibres in favour of natural materials. Clearly, she has long been ahead of the curve and her contribution to Finnish design's reputation for innovation is substantial.

Fashion has been the vehicle for much of her original thinking—but she is not a fashion designer. She learnt about sculptural form through her studies in ceramic art at the Institute of Industrial Arts in Helsinki. In addition to designing for Marimekko, she launched her own label, Vuokko, in 1964. She now lives and works in her Helsinki home, which was designed by her late husband, the architect and designer Antti Nurmesniemi.

RESOLUTELY ORIGINAL
VUOKKO NURMESNIEMI

What are the influences of the Vuokko Nurmesniemi label?
When I finished my formal education at 16, I applied to the Ateneum Institute of Industrial Arts [now the Aalto University School of Arts, Design and Architecture]. We had the finest teachers. Runar Engblom and Arttu Brummer were the school's soul, drilling into us the importance of avoiding the easy route, but rather creating and thinking for ourselves. Lighting designer Yki Nummi studied scenography at the time and painted the most wonderful, floaty aquarelles. Our teacher Beda Närhi noticed how much I admired his work and told me: 'You don't need to create the way he does, but the way you do.' She made me see. It's never been difficult for me to create since.

How did you find the courage to hold on to those words and trust yourself?
My parents taught me never to fear, which is something I've been thankful for many times. Also my uncle was an artist, who made a great impression on me. He, for instance, painted a female figure at the bottom of his bathtub and made me see another way of life. I don't have fear, but I do think carefully about what I'm about to do. My mother died when I was 14 and I became the carer for my sister and brother, which of course had an impact on my life.

Initially you studied ceramic art. How did you become skilled in textile design?
During my time at Ateneum, I also studied at the Helsinki Cutting Institute. I'm not quite sure why and I didn't even try to get any good grades, but the studies gave me skills in cutting, pattern-making and sewing. However, ceramics was the most important field for me, as it taught me all about form. After all, my clothing is as simple as can be.

Do you consider yourself a fashion designer?
No. I hate that. I call myself a designer. My designs are timeless pieces that go beyond trends and tastes; they aren't fashion. In the beginning I was making just 50 metres, by hand, of a fabric. Now, 40 years later, 26,000 metres have been produced by Marimekko.

How did you become a designer for Marimekko?
Armi Ratia called Antti [Nurmesniemi, the designer who she later married] after they'd worked on a project together, asking him to send his girlfriend over. Armi never knew that I had already tried to sell my designs to Marimekko. When I started, Armi gave me three metres of fabulous fabric designed by Viola Gråsten and told me to copy it. I'd learned that I shouldn't copy and decided to create something else: the Tibet fabric. Armi didn't say anything when I showed it to her, but I could see that something clicked. Those large-scale prints changed the whole world.

Were you ever worried about how your clothes would be received by the public?
I never thought like that. I always had a strong feeling that I have something to give.

Why are you so uncompromising?
When you ask yourself, you find the answer. I've tried to foster my own answers quite relentlessly, that's true. A piece of clothing is a piece of clothing, not fashion as such. I've never succumbed to compromises in my designs. I've treated any mistakes along the way as a learning curve that drives me forward.

Above, right and following page
The house where Vuokko Nurmesniemi lives was designed by her late husband, the industrial designer Antti Nurmesniemi. He particularly enjoyed working with metal and is most renowned for his Wärtsilä coffee pot.

Have you aimed to become international through your uncommercial and unique style?
Never. It just happened, thanks to Marimekko's world exhibitions and the Venice Bienniales, I suppose. Armi Ratia was brilliant at marketing.

You and Antti were a strong team. What were your roles? Did you critique each other's work?
Antti always worked independently. As he used to say, I took care of the soft and he of the hard work. We supported each other in spirit, but never with a guiding hand.

What roles do intuition and logic play in your designs?
I analyse my work very critically and I proceed logically. But the Chopin fabric series I created while listening to Chopin's music was more a reflection of my spiritual rather than my analytic side, which is partially based on technique and its potential. At the time, I decided to let loose and those eight Letters to Chopin were the result.

So what does inspire you?
I take a pen and paper and I study things in that way. But I never think that I should be Balenciaga, for example. I never think that I should take something from him or from what he did, although he was my big hero. I think that he is one of the few who I ever have hoped I could see. He was so his own character. But then we also had a very good design tradition in Finland.

How are your Finnish roots and nature reflected in your work?
The role of my Finnish roots can't be avoided as I was born here. They need to be reflected. I also have some Finnish role models. I've spoken about the meaning of nature since 1964, when I gave a long talk on how everything is interconnected and how human beings cannot be separated from nature. In 1986, I stopped using plastic and would no longer make clothes from acrylic. Since then, I've only used natural fibres in my work and paper bags at the shop.

Who are your role models?
I admire Tapio Wirkkala, who was the most creative of all, always developing things and treading his own path. I also admire Mies van der Rohe, the great minimalist. I appreciate the humane philosophy of Alvar Aalto, who understood the character of wood. And Eileen Gray, Le Corbusier's assistant, who designed a house that Corbusier wished he had designed himself. Who does what has been important to me, I guess, ever since that decision not to copy the Viola Gråsten pattern.

What would you say have been your key designs?
I think maybe the first lot; the Tibet print especially. It's so mystical, something like Tibet, and I find there is still some life in there. It was 1953. It was my first. Because the print was so big, they told me they could not do it. I asked why and solved the problem. But it was not what I was asked to make, this big print. So Tibet was the beginning, and I have been following that philosophy ever since.

What about the stripes?
I was making stripes before Marimekko. I made them first in 1948 when I was studying. I think the stripes are very rhythmical. There is something about me in the stripes.

Would you say you are an individual thinker?
In Finland, sometimes, some people are small. They cannot think big. This is because we have always been living small. I understood that something like the Guggenheim should be very good for us. The small Finnish artists and people thought, 'Oh we cannot have it, it's too big and expensive', and so on. They don't understand that we are living in the future, not today.

Above
Tibet 1952 Marimekko.

Opposite left
Designer Tapio Wirkkala was one of the very first to wear a Jokapoika shirt. Sporting one today remains a statement: a suggestion that the wearer is part of a cultural elite. Nurmesniemi designed the shirt in 1956 and it has been in production ever since.

Opposite right
Lounge chairs 1970 by Antti Nurmesniemi and covered in a characteristic stripe fabric by Vuokko Nurmesniemi.

DESIGNER AND INDUSTRY

The role of my Finnish roots can't be avoided as I was born here. They need to be reflected.

VUOKKO NURMESNIEMI

Viima dress made from Jokiraita fabric 1967.

I made stripes first in 1948 when I was studying. I think they are very rhythmical. There is something about me in the stripes.

VUOKKO NURMESNIEMI

Hooded dress made from Purje fabric 1973.

Ville Kokkonen is design director of Artek, Finland's most iconic furniture-maker and the brand that for many most efficiently illustrates the special relationship between design, industry and social innovation. Being the custodian of the Artek legacy involves much more than simply maintaining its back catalogue of celebrated designs. The innovative thinking and idealistic principles of its four founders—Alvar and Aino Aalto, Maire Gullichsen and Nils-Gustav Hahl—still guide Artek's newest projects as it advances out of Finland and into Europe.

The idea that a furniture-maker can be an educator and an innovator, as well as a producer of chairs and lighting, continues to inspire such ground-breaking new products as White Lights. Other imaginative explorations by Artek in recent years include new material innovations, such as the recycled composite used in the 10-Unit System by Shigeru Ban; an experimentation with production and the self-made via Enzo Mari's Sedia 1 Chair; the launch of a new publishing arm and the opening of a Second Cycle store.

ALL OUR FUTURES
ARTEK

Artek has never been just a simple furniture-making company, has it?
When Artek was founded in 1935, Aino and Alvar Aalto, and also Maire Gullischsen and Nils-Gustav Hahl, had this idea that it would not just be a company that sells a lot of furniture. They had a bigger idea that Artek should be a centre of information regarding art and design, and higher culture in that sense. In the founding manifesto it says that Artek should be a 'propaganda centre for new housing ideology', which was quite advanced at that time. And they also had Galerie Artek, where they held the first Picasso show in Finland. The furniture wasn't designed to be super-exclusive. First and foremost it had to be affordable to mass produce, which was the founders' goal.

How difficult is it to maintain the original principles in a modern company?
We looked at this closely when Artek turned 75. We took education as a theme in our agenda. Rather than just investing in new products, we thought that we should have a few projects that have an educational aspect. As a direct result we worked with Enzo Mari's Autoprogettazione and Sedia 1 chair.

If you draw a financial chart this may not make any sense. But these projects have a different kind of value for us and ultimately to our clients. Also, companies like us that have a legacy to take care of often have a wide portfolio of products. We still maintain production of some of our unique items that don't sell that much. If we were just a company seeking profit, then we would certainly stop making them and just keep them in the posters.

What about innovation and keeping things moving forward?
In order for us to be active, alive and up-to-date with what's going on in the world it is important for us to reach for the new. And really to think of tomorrow's problems as more than, 'How many pieces can we sell and what colour shall we have it in?' I try to see how circumstances change, how people work in offices, how they live at home, and what they do in their pastime.

Since we're a small company, we can act really quickly and produce projects that answer some questions about changing needs. We invest time into research and we benefit from the fact that Finland has quite an open system with university collaborations.

You seem to allow time for projects that need to be done well. Is that part of the Artek culture too?
Yes. I think that our team is really privileged in that.

Is there anything in Artek's success that is particular to its being a Finnish company?
Yes. That's a good question—although it is very difficult to answer. We have a great legacy here that was built by people who travelled the world and recognised that there is tough competition out there. They managed because of that.

Above
Ville Kokkonen.

Right
Kokkonen tackled the dark Finnish winters head on with his design for Bright Lights. The Bright White 1 table lamp is certified bright-light therapy, designed to ease seasonal affective disorder (SAD), and is typical of Kokkonen's human-centred approach to design.

> **Since we're small company, we can act really quickly and produce projects that answer some questions about changing needs.**
>
> VILLE KOKKONEN

What causes that lack of ambition?
I think they are too much in a comfort zone of some sort. I find that it's the Finnish engineers who are the people that I really want to work with, some of whom are very ambitious in inventing things such as future materials. There is one particularly interesting material being developed here: a liquid malleable glass that is as strong as steel and a fraction of the price. It's very exciting.

But to come back to your question, I saw that spirit of ambition in the founders of this company. Nowadays it is less apparent here in Finland. I think we have been maybe focusing too much on a Finnish campaign. The only way for us to survive is to go out to where the clients are, somewhere other than Finland.

Alvar Aalto spoke about being part of a small community of artists and architects. That close creative community here in Finland is often seen in a positive light. But from what you have just said, can it also be a limiting thing?
Yes, I'm sure. I have a feeling that some of the Finnish designers think that the competition is really difficult outside Finland or that you have to succeed here first. But it shouldn't be like that.

How do you choose which past pieces to bring on to the market again? How do you decide if they are fit for contemporary purpose?
For example, Lukki, the tubular steel chair that we're now launching was produced in the 1950s. It never went into mass production so it is of great interest to see it realised now. Sometimes it is purely the fact that it's easier for us to make moulds and produce some of the pieces now than it was in the past. And some decisions are based on the fact that we recognise that there's a need for more playful chairs. We're involved with many kindergarten projects, for example.

Part of me thinks that bringing these classics back, or reintroducing them, gives a stronger picture of the company. It shows that we have these archives. Ultimately it's not necessarily a financial decision: it's that we want people to be able to buy these things. Plus there is an awareness of the vintage business, demonstrated in our Second Cycle project. We are often asked: 'Will this come to production?' It's important that we have a story, a link to a piece of architecture or to a history.

Clockwise, from right
Shelf System low unit 2009 by Naoto Fukasawa.

10-Unit System chair 2009 by Shigeru Ban.

Sedia 1 Chair 1974 by Enzo Mari, reintroduced 2010.

Lukki Series 1951–56 by Ilmari Tapiovaara, reintroduced 2013.

Pirkka Series 1955 by Ilmari Tapiovaara, reintroduced 2009.

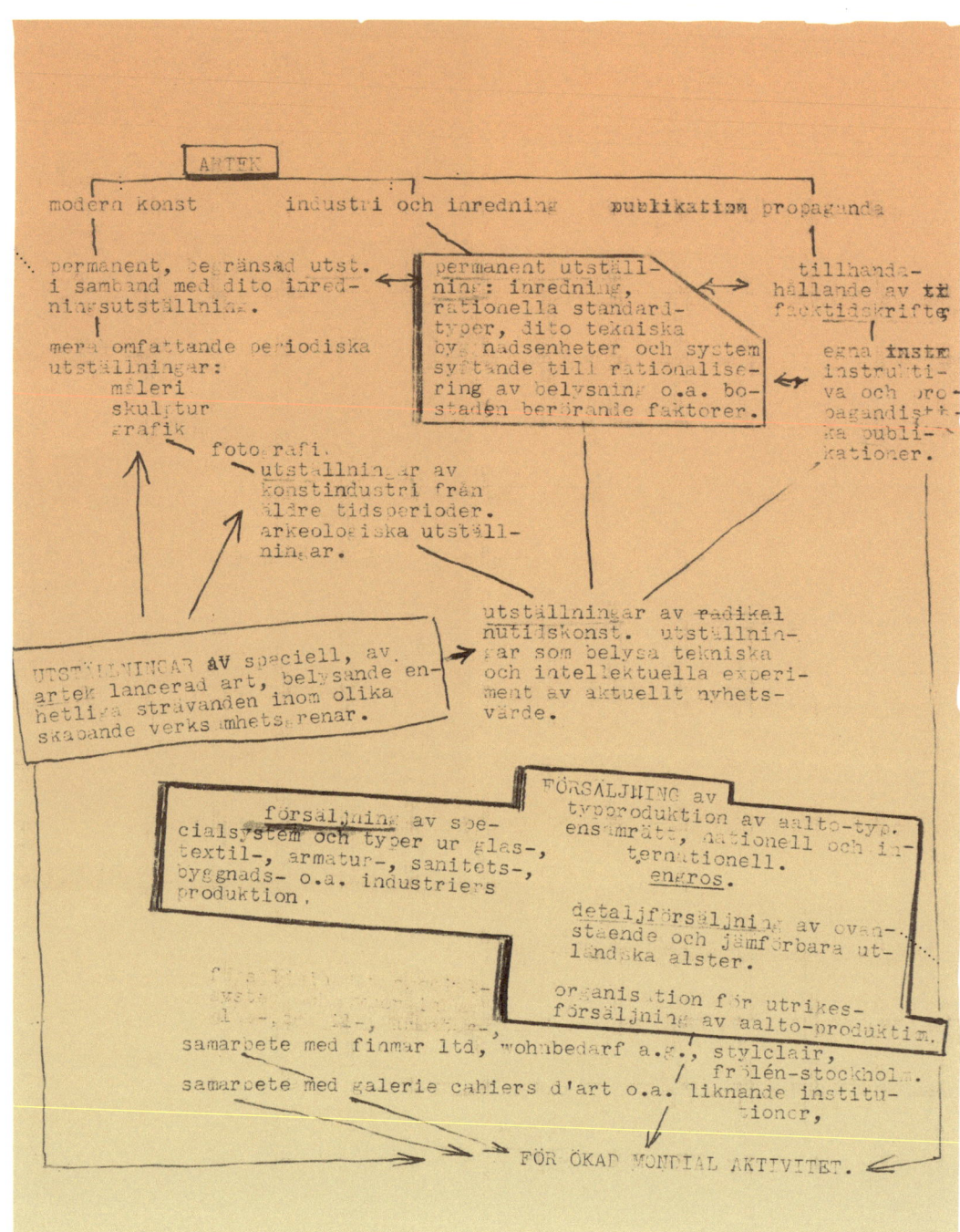

In the founding manifesto it says that Artek was to be a 'propaganda centre for new housing ideology'.

VILLE KOKKONEN

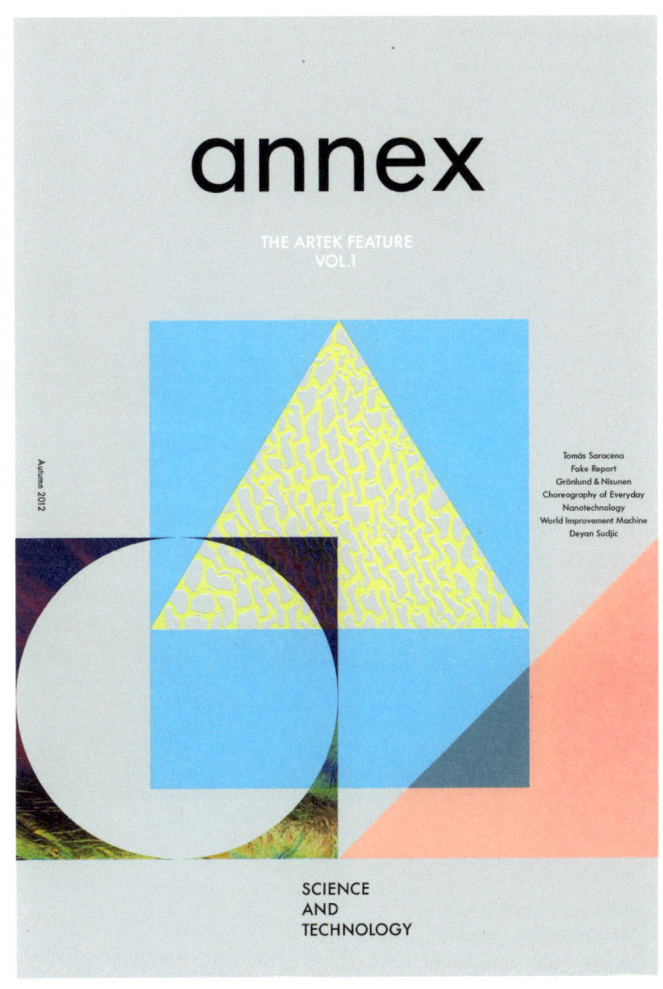

Opposite page
This irreverent manifesto, seemingly hastily sketched by the founders of Artek, is actually a blueprint for a grand synthesis of the arts. They wanted to bring about improvements in everyday urban life as well as in architecture and design. The vision was to connect modern visual arts, rational furniture production and popular education.

This page
Artek promotional material has always been clear and graphic.

Bottom right
The recent publication of Annex magazine reaffirms the brand's original commitment to communication and education.

The home of a collector of Artek and other modern classic furniture from celebrated designers such as Charles and Ray Eames and Le Corbusier.

This nomadic pavilion, designed by Shigeru Ban, was created for exhibition at the Milan Salone del Mobile and subsequently shown at design events such as Design Miami. It was filled with 100 used Aalto chairs. This unconventional piece of ecological architecture demonstrated Artek's attitude toward sustainable development, while underlining the brand's ongoing dialogue between design, architecture and art.

The A808 brass floor lamp 1955 by Alvar Aalto is shown above. Another 1950s lighting solution is the A110 pendant lamp 1952, right. The original is shown here, although the A110 was recently updated with a new colour palette by Mike Meiré.

The Paimio chair 1932 by Alvar Aalto. It still surprises some people to learn that the elegant and covetable Paimio chair was for use by the ill and frail residents of the Paimio Sanatorium.

The X-Leg table 1954 by Alvar Aalto. A handsome example of how Aalto used manufacturing detail as an aesthetic device.

Stool 60 1933 by Alvar Aalto. 'We'll make thousands of these one day!' was Aalto's considerable understatement on creating the simple bent wood Stool 60. It pioneered a unique bending technology, later patented, and remains the most widely recognised, and used, of his furniture.

Behind an inconspicuous entrance, hidden beneath a Helsinki street, lies the Artek Second Cycle store. The shop is the commercial face of a preservation project that Artek began several years ago. Galvanised by the growing interest in vintage Artek designs, the company began to buy back its own second-hand furniture from schools, institutions and individuals. Today, the Second Cycle store is a subterranean nirvana for furniture aficionados and collectors.

> It's important that we have a story, a link to a piece of architecture or to a history.
>
> **VILLE KOKKONEN**

'Design culture' is a rarely used term at Nokia. That's because design simply is our culture and has been for as long as we can remember. When we do reflect on our design identity, it's impossible to ignore our Finnish-ness. It has always coloured our approach. We speak of our communication devices and experiences as pure, human and 'built better', and the origin of these qualities is a set of values that maintain an honest approach to materials and processes. We make technology a human concern and we're dedicated to craft and attention to detail.

These values and design motivations have their roots in Finland and in Finnish culture, but are expressed by an international team of designers and engineers working in studios across the world. These designers create the hardware, software and packaging for products that sell in the hundreds of millions every year. On the following pages, a few key Nokia designers discuss a little more about what they do, and how and why they do it.

PRODUCT OF FINLAND
NOKIA

THIS IS WHAT WE DO

Nokia Design is deeply involved in the physical making of phones and tablets, of course, but its work doesn't stop there. Its team of designers spend their days imagining how to make the experience of getting from here to there easier with HERE Maps; wondering what the best way is to keep our 'heads up'; and defining when, exactly, the curve on a phone is just round enough to make it pleasurable to hold.

A seemingly obvious question, perhaps, but what does Nokia make?

Stefan: We build absolutely fantastic communication devices. And we create absolutely fantastic communication experiences. The notion of communication has changed quite significantly over the short history of Nokia's involvement in the industry.[1] You could argue that the way people communicate these days reflects social change. So, in a way, that is the business we are in.

How does being Finnish affect the character of the brand, in broad terms?

Rhys: Nokia is uniquely and powerfully Finnish. Beliefs and values such as authenticity, respect and democracy are at the core of the company. It's a symbol of modern Finland and of European high-tech. Our values and culture make Nokia a great platform for positive impact.

Axel: The culture of the company is very Finnish: it is open, horizontal, maybe sometimes too much so. There is a way of relating to your colleagues that you don't find in many other companies. Such as discussing things in the sauna or rolling in the snow. If employees aren't Finnish they are a little shocked.

Stefan: There is a certain pragmatic streak to the Finns, pragmatic in the best sense. There is also a mindset that wants to do good for society: that's commonplace. Finland has a very democratic, open-minded culture and this impacts our work in all kinds of ways.

And how does that impact on what you do at Nokia? How do those kind of values affect the way you work?

Stefan: We listen to employees and they feel respected. They voice their opinion freely without worrying about the impact. Pragmatism also affects how we design and the judgments we make. Humility and perseverance are common Finnish characteristics and they are certainly part of Nokia's character too.

Nikki: If you look at Finnish culture and design, there is a purity to it and a clarity, a taking away of the unnecessary to get to the core of a design. That is key to the industrial design of the Nokia devices we make and the user experience too.

Peter S: And there is one value that is fundamentally Finnish: integrity. There is a refusal to engage in behaviour that evades responsibility; a point where empathy meets accountability.

What shifts has the brand gone through over the years?

Nikki: Nokia is a company that has always been open to change. It was a paper mill originally, then it made tyres and rubber boots, then TVs[2] and then mobile phones. Which is why now is so interesting: the company is again going through one of its biggest evolutions.

Where does design sit within Nokia?

Stefan: I think design has always been very much at the heart of the company. Or let's say design-like thinking and design-like attitudes have always been at the heart of the company. Nokia was the first company to treat mobile phones as pure consumer devices. I think that is a very design-minded approach: to democratise technology.

Peter G: If you look back to the time when the technical challenges of making phones were so big, all the devices were like instruments. They were pieces of raw technology, but nobody really cared about that because it was so amazing that you could carry a phone around with you. What Nokia did was to turn that technology into a design: a human device in terms of form and colour, but also in the simplicity of the user interface.

Nokia was the first to see this product as more than just technology; to see it as a personal object that people would want to own. I think that's an interesting point of origin for the objects being produced today.

What is the design studio culture like?

Peter G: The design studio is pretty diverse. A lot of people studied industrial design, but there are others, like me, who may have studied furniture design or have other backgrounds. There are people from the automotive industry and some more craft-based backgrounds. It's a very wide range of skills. And there is a massive range of nationalities.[3]

Stefan: There is room for individuals, but I think there's also a lot of room for teamwork and for working across different disciplines. I don't think many people in this organisation, if any at all, are interested in creating design for the museum. I think they're interested in creating designs that end up in the hands of people. There's an incredible commitment to detail and to doing the hard stuff; the un-glorious stuff that in the end is really important.

What is the hard stuff; the un-glorious stuff?

Stefan: The nasty little details that are quite technical or the discussions around the bill of materials. Nokia designers feel very responsible for their contribution.

Our interviewees
Axel Meyer
Nikki Barton
Peter Griffith
Peter Skillman
Rhys Newman
Stefan Pannenbecker

1. Nokia was founded as a pulp mill in 1865 in the town of Nokia in southern Finland. In 1982, it introduced the first car phone, the Mobira Senator. It made its first digital handheld GSM phone, the Nokia 1011, in 1992.

2. The full spectrum of products made by Nokia since 1865 includes paper, tyres, rubber boots, cables, personal computers, robotics, gas masks, consumer electronics, mobile phones and, believe it or not, a few other things too.

3. As of 2013 people from 32 nationalities are employed in Nokia's design studio.

Left
Research, experimentation and testing play a huge part in the studio culture of Nokia Design. Here, colour variants for a new model are examined.

Below
The Nokia Asha 210 is a phone that expresses the results of a lengthy research and development process.

Following page
The Lumia family includes smart devices such as phones, tablets and hybrids like the Nokia Lumia 1520.

Nokia was the first company to treat mobile phones as pure consumer devices. I think that is a very design-minded approach: to democratise technology.

STEFAN PANNENBECKER

Left
Colour sampling and the distinctive yellow in use on the Nokia 820 and 920 models.

Below
Prototypes of colour and finishes.

HUMAN DESIGN

Human design is something of a Nokia mantra. It reflects the belief that technology and human nature need not be contrary or conflicting; that technology can do much to help us be more human. That belief informs the way Nokia devices are conceived, evolved and made. Applying human values to technology leads to the development of intuitive and emotive systems; to labouring over details in a craft-like manner; or to creating tools that simply make their users' everyday lives a little better.

What is the relationship between technology and human nature, as seen at Nokia?

Axel: Every designer's challenge is to create a human way of interacting with the artificial environment around us. Technology is the Arts and Crafts of today's world. Where once you had a blacksmith and a carpenter creating everyday objects, now you have a couple of us trying to translate all of these innovations into something that has some meaning.

Stefan: Yes exactly, we're making technology more human. There are a couple of aspects to that. First, there is the shock of the new: a designer's job is to overcome that and to make things relevant and more meaningful. What that means for me is not just making things usable; it is about the pleasure of use. It is about putting so much love into a product that you believe it will be the last product of that kind that a person will ever want to buy. And I think that is our goal. Some people might think that is a very un-commercial way to think.

It's a romantic thought…

Stefan: Absolutely. But there is no reason to put anything out into the world if you don't believe somebody will really love it. It should be painful to let go of the product, to get the new one. It should feel like, 'Man, you know, I really love this thing!' One example of how we approach that is with our use of colour. People love their yellow phone because it is such a strong statement. People don't acquire a yellow phone by accident.

Communications are a massive part of our everyday lives. What are the areas that Nokia is especially concerned with?

Rhys: Products are getting bigger, displays have a higher resolution, and we can do more and more on them. If you look around in public places; in restaurants and at people walking down the street, they are walking with their heads down, poking and swiping at the devices we built. This is because they are designed to maximise our attention. Dealing with the consequences of that led us to a great brief: How do we design our products in a way that doesn't compromise connectivity, usability, functionality and beauty, but to be calmer, quieter and less intrusive? Essentially, how do we find ways to bring people's heads up again?

Nikki: Yeah, one great example of this is the Glance screen.[1] With the Glance screen, I don't need to switch my phone on to check the time or to see missed calls. It eliminates an everyday task, and is an example of how we are always looking to improve communication between people.

This was surprisingly complex but it works beautifully in our latest range of Lumias. It's interesting how something so simple completely changes the way you interact with your phone.

How do you see the human need to connect evolving over the coming years?

Peter S: Knowing where you are and where you're going are fundamental human needs, so location becomes increasingly important. With our HERE Maps[2], we provide beautifully relevant answers, visual answers, to everyday questions. This is all about exploring and understanding the world around you and encouraging you to go out, be mobile and enjoy a richer life. We can help you see what is inside a building, find out what time your bus is coming or where to eat dinner. But our biggest interest is in how you experience and contextualise this information.

Stefan: The phone is the physical result of the technical capabilities that we have. But if those capabilities change then a phone may be obsolete.

Interactions that dissolve into behaviour are something we're working on. Swiping is a very conscious act. And you could argue that ultimately we should overcome that. Some of our accessories[3] allow the functions of the phone to exist away from the actual device. And I think that is another idea of how communication being integrated into the environment around us will become more interesting in the future.

Peter S: Exactly, what matters is that the experience you are having transfers seamlessly between increasing numbers of connected devices.

Tell me about where the physical and digital worlds meet and why this is an important consideration.

Peter G: I think this is a very key area. We have an industrial design team working on the physical objects and right next to them the digital design team is working on the user interface.

There are a few areas where the two cross. One example is when we match colour between the displays and the phones. Nokia has a portfolio that runs from €15 to €600s[4], but we go to great lengths to be consistent on all models. In the early stages of a product we'll get hold of the LCD display, wire it up on a breadboard[5] and render colour on it. Then the people that are working on the polycarbonate shell will be able to compare plastic samples with an accurate LCD colour rendering. Sometimes it's easier to adjust the properties of the display screen; sometimes you need to adjust the mix of the resin colour. It seems so basic from the outside but to do it really well involves in-depth work.

---

1. The Glance screen is a low-power mode feature and is available on all Lumia models.

2. HERE Maps is a comprehensive index of information that is gathered, monthly, by 20 billion probes.

3. Nokia's accessories collection includes headsets, speakers and wireless charging equipment.

4. Nokia's most affordable phone is the Nokia 105 at €15 and its most expensive is the Nokia Lumia 1020 at €600.

5. A breadboard is a working model that designers use in early stages of prototyping.

Stefan: We believe that the world is noisy enough and these objects should be visually simple and unobtrusive. The moment you turn a phone on, the actual object itself should move into the background. This should be a beautiful object when it's on the table and when you hold it in your hand. But nobody looks at a TV once the TV is on. They look at what happens on the screen. That's the same for the objects that we create. We need to make sure that nothing distracts from what happens on our product's screen when you are using it.

We encourage that by creating an almost seamless design. Because of the way the glass is curved, when you swipe it is a really pleasant experience. That is just one area where the digital and physical reinforce each other.

Axel: Humanness has a lot to do with interaction and the way we relate to objects. Industrial design is most successful when it makes the experience the important thing and doesn't try to be to the centre of attention.

Human Design can also refer to the significance of the human in the design process. Is that a consideration at Nokia?
Stefan: You could look at phone design as being straightforward: just create a box, stuff all the technology in there and be as space efficient as possible and make it as cheap as possible. And that would be rational. But we are irrational sometimes. We sculpt these phones to be soft, to sit gently in the hand, and we include details like a slightly curved glass which makes the product a little bit more expensive. It is an irrational thing to do, but it results in a craft-like quality. When you look at a Nokia product, you don't think that it comes from an assembly line. It looks and feels like a more natural, more poetic process of product creation was involved here.

So Human Design, in Nokia terms, can also refer to the explicitness of the human hand in the product's making?
Stefan: Yes. And then of course human design also means that, when we paint our products, which we do less and less, we use water-based colours, or that the internal components are made in such a way that they have as low an impact as possible on the environment. Nokia is one of the greenest companies.

Top right
The Glance screen, shown here on the Nokia Asha 501, allows users to access basic information, such as the time, without having to switch on their device.

Bottom right
Lower-range mobile phones, such as the Nokia 105, 301, 206 and Nokia Asha 210, make use of the innovative production techniques first developed for higher-price devices. It shows Nokia's desire to democratise technology.

We provide beautifully relevant answers, visual answers, to everyday questions.

PETER SKILLMAN

Above
Nokia designers put the 'human' at the forefront of what they do.

Right
In an increasingly digital world, tactility is becoming more important than ever before. The pleasing way a Nokia Lumia gently sits in the hand is just one way a human element is brought into Nokia's design language.

Above
LiveSight, a HERE Maps feature, helps the user navigate using a topological view of the world around them.

Left
HERE, a Nokia business, offers personalised maps, navigation and public transport information with an advanced hybrid architecture that allows customers to avoid expensive roaming charges while travelling.

Right
The designers of hardware and software both need to rapidly prototype and visualise design solutions. The user interface is where hardware and software meet, and the heart of any user interface is the mental model. These design diagrams depict the mental models of user interfaces for the Nokia N9 and the Nokia Asha family of affordable smartphones.

NOKIA ASHA

NOKIA N9

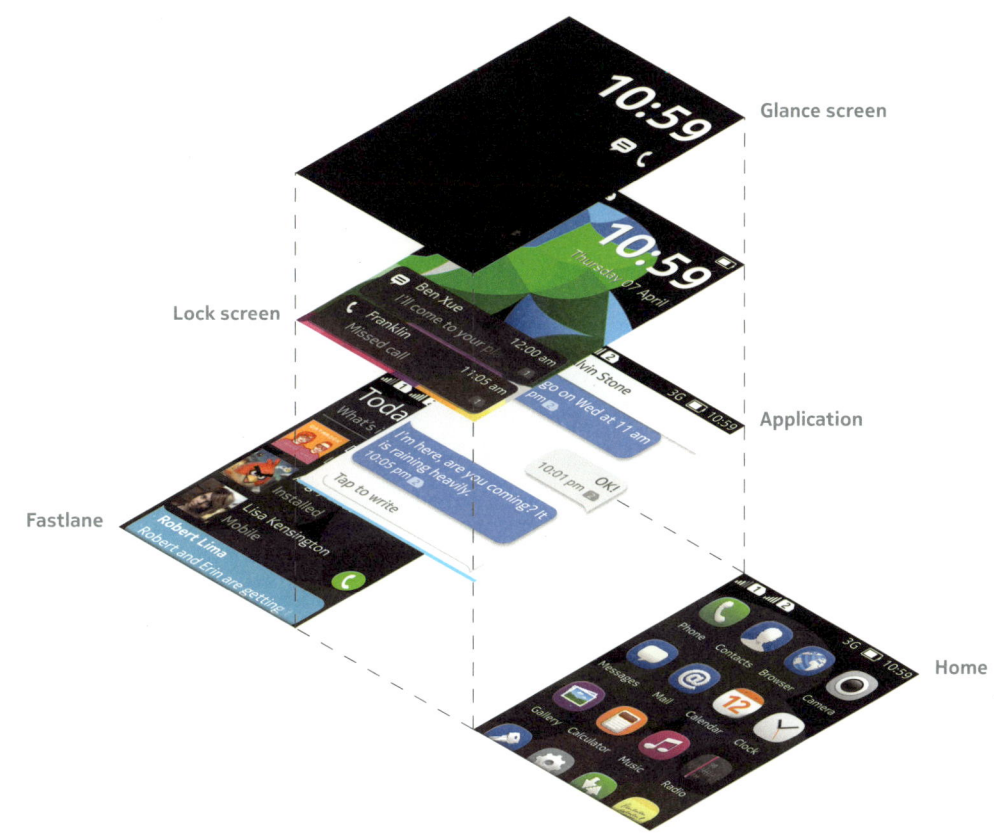

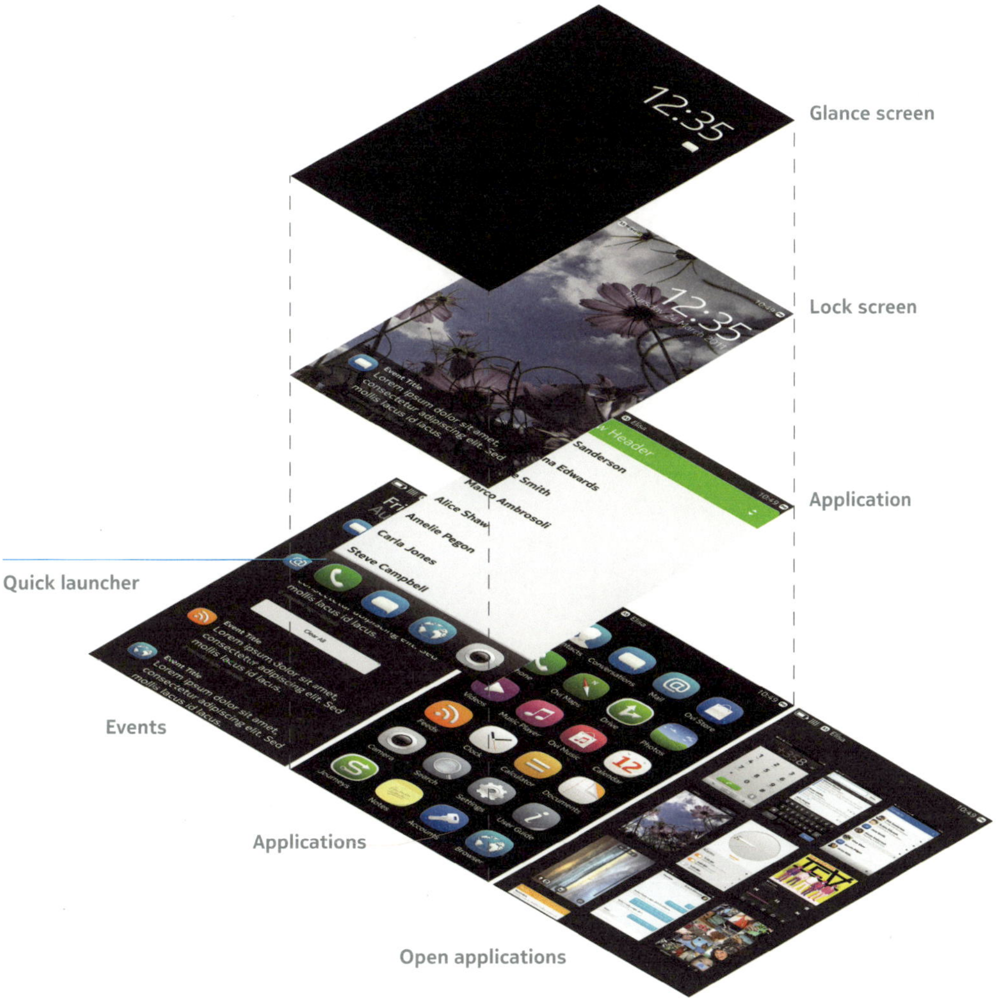

PURE DESIGN

An honest approach to materials and process is characteristic of Nokia's design. There is no 'small talk' here. It is relentlessly reductive, stripping away all that's unnecessary so that only the essential forms, systems, materials and information remain. Uncluttered and unencumbered by fashions or trends, the Nokia way of making things is intuitive, direct and no-nonsense.

Tell me about the Nokia approach to materials. How has this changed and why?
Stefan: We have a materials-based design approach. Which means that we're always thinking about what a material can do and designing towards those capabilities.

I imagine that once you began that method of thinking, it was impossible to go back.
Stefan: If I walked into a room and said, 'OK, that's great, but let's slap some metal on this thing,' our designers would look at me like I'm crazy. They'd ask, 'Why would we do that? What is the reasoning behind it?' Absolutely, this way of working creates a strong value system. And that creates the identity, ultimately, of a consistent portfolio.

What made you settle on polycarbonate as a signature material?
Peter G: Plastic is such a familiar, commonplace material and we were looking for a material with radio frequency transparency, and polycarbonate, along with glass and very few other materials, is excellent. For us, the material is integral to designing an efficient, innovative product.

What results has polycarbonate given you?
Peter G: It gave us the monobody design, which is an important innovation and used across our Lumia family.[1] Plastic is a great material because you can injection-mould it into almost any shape. We then found that, if we used machines originally designed for cutting metal and slowed the speeds down, we could cut the plastic very effectively and with a high level of precision. We got more out of injection moulding by this post-processing, and from this evolved an approach for the whole portfolio of objects.

How does this 'honest' approach to materials reflect a wider ethos?
Peter G: This is about understanding what is the best material we can make an object from, and what is the best we can do with it. I have a Tapio Wirkkala quote that is very useful: 'Material always entails opportunities. It's as if it urges one to create something out of it.' He had a way of conversing with a material and understanding its properties. There are some things a material lends itself to and some things it doesn't. And if you work with this you will get a beautiful result.

Is there an equivalent to that materials story with the user interface? Is there a similar way of thinking?
Nikki: We have an honest approach. We make things simple to use while being very advanced at the same time. We strip out the unnecessary and keep what is practical and beautiful.

What made you choose CMYK colours for Lumia products?
Peter G: As we were experimenting with materials and polycarbonate, we decided to stop applying colour with paint and started using the resin itself as the colour. The pigment is the material and the material is the pigment. It's no accident that we ended up with CMYK[2] as a palette. When CMD[3] did a study, they found that these worked best because they are the process colours. We used colour in this way for the first time with the N9 and the Lumia 800. CMYK made a lot of sense in terms of making the brand more recognisable.

Nikki: The inherent colour means that if you scratch or drop your device the colour doesn't come off. The colours we used initially were cyan, magenta, yellow and black, the 'key' colour. And then we started to introduce other colours such as the red in the Lumia 920, which is a mix of those initial pure colours. It is very satisfying, this consistency of approach between the industrial design, the digital design and the colours.

1. The monobody, a two-part construction that improves structural strength and robustness, was first used on the Nokia N9 in 2011. The polycarbonate monobody is used widely in Nokia's portfolio, but there are exceptions, such as the evolutionary Nokia Lumia 925, which has a metal band running around its middle.

2. CMYK stands for cyan, magenta, yellow and the 'key' colour, which is black. CMYK is a process-colour model used frequently in colour printing.

3. CMD is the Colour and Material Design team within Nokia Design.

Following pages:
Left
Nokia has exploited the natural properties of polycarbonate in its monobody designs. The material's fluidity, toughness and ability to hold colour have been a great inspiration. An evolution of the monobody is the 'crystal clear' finish: a layer of coloured polycarbonate covered by a clear resin.

Right above
Colour has become an important expression at Nokia. The original CMYK palette was recently extended to include an additional range of colours.

Right below
Nokia accessories include the Purity Pro Wireless Stereo Headset, Nokia Luna Bluetooth Headset and JBL PlayUp Portable Wireless Speaker. The accessories extend the functions of a Nokia phone into a wider environment.

> We have a materials-based design approach. Which means that we're always thinking about what a material can do and designing towards those capabilities.
>
> STEFAN PANNENBECKER

BUILT BETTER

There is a work ethic in the Nokia Design Studio that focuses on the principles of perseverance and quality. In many ways, some of the design decisions are illogical: for example, drilling holes takes longer and creating curved glass costs more. Yet they are made because everyone believes that a better-quality product and a better-quality experience will come of it. It is a craft-like mentality that Nokia enjoys, which is an unusual concession for a technology brand to make.

How is Nokia's approach to manufacturing different to that of other technology brands?
Stefan: We spend a lot of time on research and investigation and we strive to build better, meaning we really live in the details and try to find the best way to manufacture things. So, in a sense, a designer needs to be a little bit of an engineer as well. We need to be interested in the areas that are outside our traditional core capabilities.

Peter G: Being a furniture designer originally gave me a certain way of looking at the world. I think how we work at Nokia is very similar to that. The very best production technologies and processes today are difficult to master: they require skill. There is a clear element of 'the hand' present in what we do, whether that's working out the progressive stamping of this part, the machining of that, or producing the monobody. It wouldn't work if we simply drew a shape and then handed it over to the engineers and said, 'OK, make this'. They would then produce an approximation. Understanding how a production line works is the same level of understanding that you would need if you were working in a workshop and just making one or two.

Craft and industrial design aren't so far apart. Maybe this is where design fits into the contemporary world. We are making that connection between how something is conceived, how it's built and how we use it. Interestingly, the digital design team at Nokia talk about pixels as if they were physical things as well. Like building blocks.

What are the areas where being built better really makes a substantial difference?
Peter G: My entire team gets up every morning, comes to work and designs mobile phones. We do the same thing over and over again, but that creates an opportunity. Every time we do it, we do it a little bit better than last time. That led to this idea of 'built better'.

Now we even treat what happens beneath the hood of a phone as another user interface. See this line that runs around the edge? That is a drip groove: it stops water from getting into the key parts. We wanted to make it symmetrical. If the user sees that line then let's make it look right. We worked on the design and position of the label, which meant that we had to collaborate with care centres and with international distribution, among many other things.

It led us to be able to make a better user experience, in every small way. That's another very Finnish principle. Alvar Aalto said, 'The architect's task is to provide a gentler structure for life.'

In other words, bettering the everyday experience?
Peter G: Yes, for us, the impact of what we do translates into a better-quality experience in those things that you do many, many times a day. There's always a temptation in a competitive market to be doing something that's really big and impactful. But the things that really matter are the things that people do many times a day. The results of our design work can be very subtle and maybe you don't even notice them. In this respect, the Lumia 800[1] was an absolute milestone in terms of where Nokia is today.

Nikki: The creation of the Nokia Pure font[2] is a good example of attention to detail in user interfaces too; it really is key to the experience. In designing a digital font you need to be very aware of how many pixels there are to play with. You have to get the proportions right, have letters that work well together, but that are easily recognisable as separate forms. You need to look carefully at the width of each letter, the rendering of the font on screen and what the software allows you to do. And, of course, the end result should be so good that the user doesn't notice it.

How important is the consideration of how your customer interacts with their communication devices?
Peter S: We rethink the experience to make it relevant and personal. Providing a quality experience is important, but we need to have an emotional relationship with our users beyond utility. They need to trust the product. And that comes down to the details. As a brand we could do more of the 'shiny things' that might get attention, but we are interested in making the best quality experiences we can.

The challenges of software are very different to those of industrial design. Sometimes even a 30-millisecond delay matters, so you have to be obsessive about the detail. Here, performance isn't just a feature, sometimes it's the only feature.

Stefan: We aim for seamlessness in the physical product, but also in tasks such as charging a product or exchanging content via NFC (near field communication), where the physical act of two devices touching each other actually represents and initiates an exchange of information. We have these almost gestural, real-world interactions replacing the pushing of buttons. And, of course, the phone demonstrates a similar kind of attitude towards form-giving in the digital space to what we have in the physical space.

How does the way you work influence your offering?
Peter G: Building consistency across the whole portfolio has added a great inherent strength on many levels. Each individual device is drawing from the same small group of details.

1. The Nokia Lumia 800 was the first Nokia phone to use the Windows Phone.

2. Nokia Pure is a bespoke font developed by Dalton Maag for Nokia. The new font family had to reflect the traditions of Finnish design: simplicity, clarity, functionality, beauty of form. It is currently used only on Nokia's mobile phones.

Nikki: The Nokia accessories collection is an example of how the family of Nokia products is extended and how the idea of the functions of what we do exist beyond the device. Examples are the Luna Bluetooth Headset or the PlayUp Portable Wireless Speaker. You can extend the phone experiences, as we do with Mix Radio[3], across different hardware products.

Stefan: There are many great products, all sharing common values. From products like the Lumia 720, which although relatively low cost has all the characteristics of this recent generation of Nokia products, to the 206[4]. You could say the colour or the material is the point of interest with the 206, but it's almost impossible to put your finger on what makes it so particular. There is a unifying idea, and a fearlessness, behind all these products.

Above
Speaker holes and headphone jack details from Nokia Asha and Lumia devices displaying superior-quality finish.

Right
The back of a phone is treated as another user interface and great care is paid to the visual impact of even the most minor technical details.

3. Mix Radio is a free music streaming service that is available exclusively on all Nokia Lumia smartphones.

4. The Nokia 206 is an accessible low-cost feature phone. It makes the seamlessness, purity and craft reminiscent of the Lumia devices available to those who choose a simpler phone.

Along with our interviewees we would like to thank some more people from the Nokia Design Studio: Andrew Gartrell, Anton Fahlgren, Benoit Rouger, Joakim Karske, Joeske Schellen, Jonne Harju, Juhani Haaparanta, Luke Johnson, Nicola Ralston, Niilo Alfthan, Raun Forsyth, Roope Rainisto, Shunjiro Eguchi, Sondre Ager-Wick, Stephen White, Tapio Hakanen, Timo-Pekka Viljamaa and Ulla Uimonen.

> We treat what happens beneath the hood of a phone as another user interface.
>
> PETER GRIFFITH

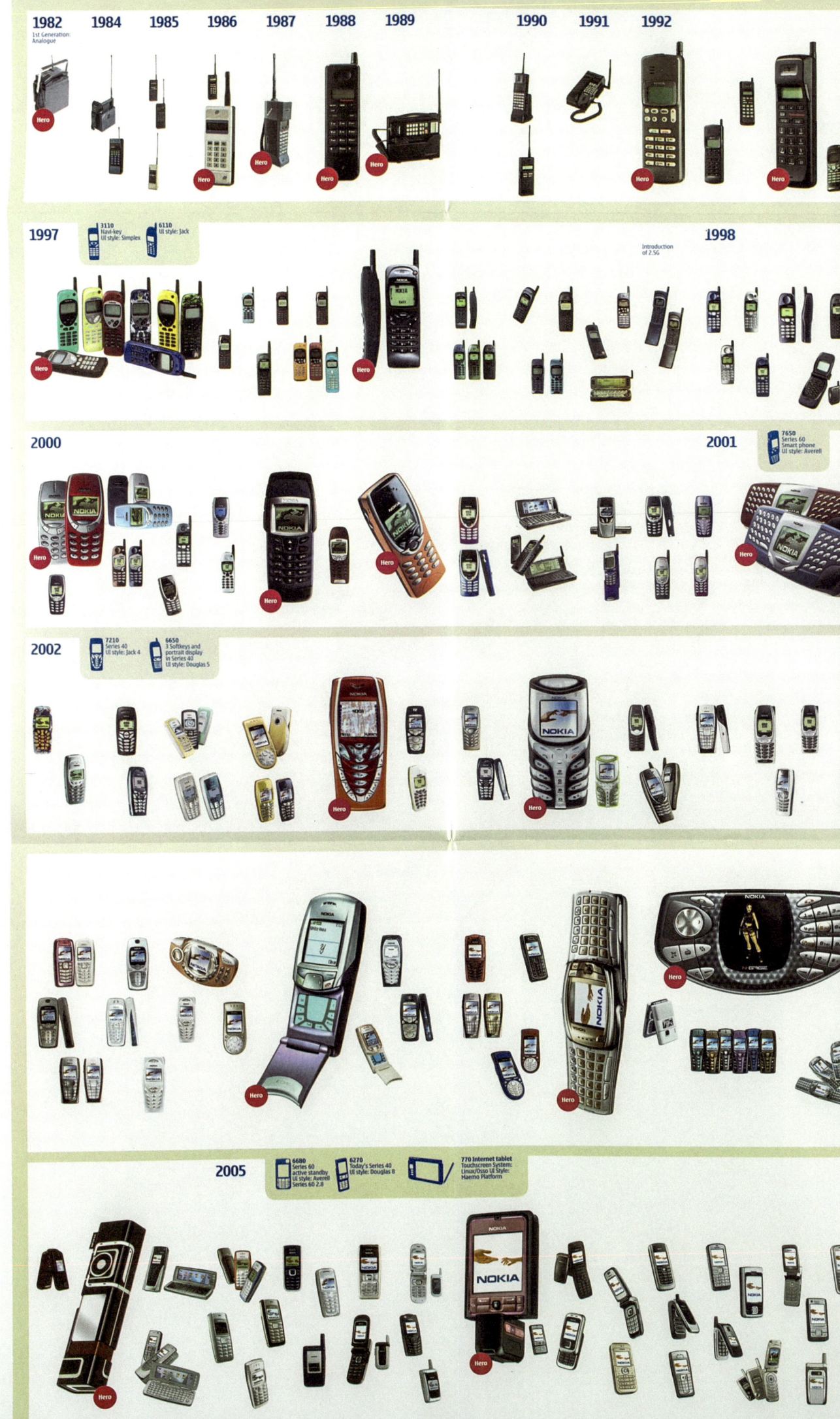

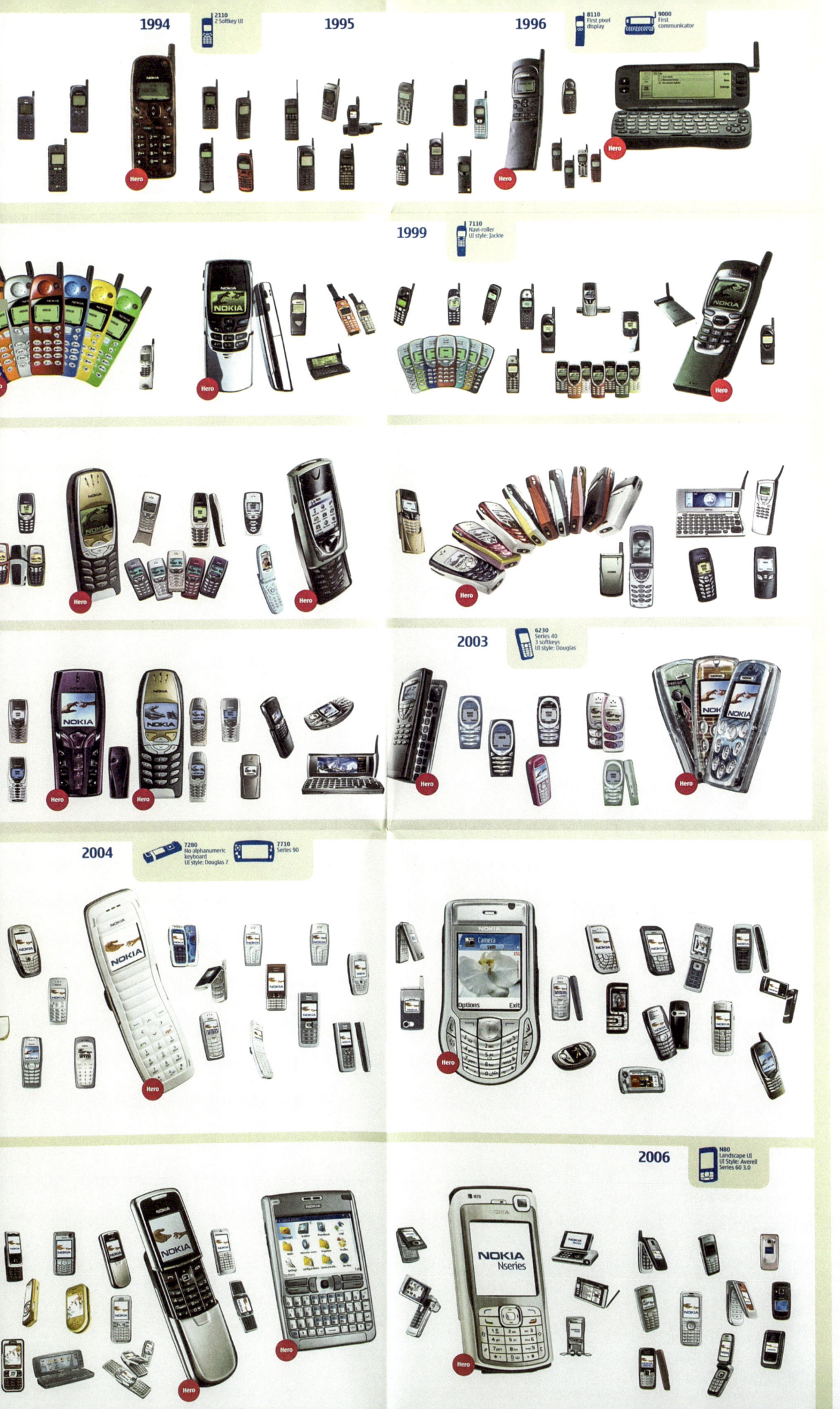

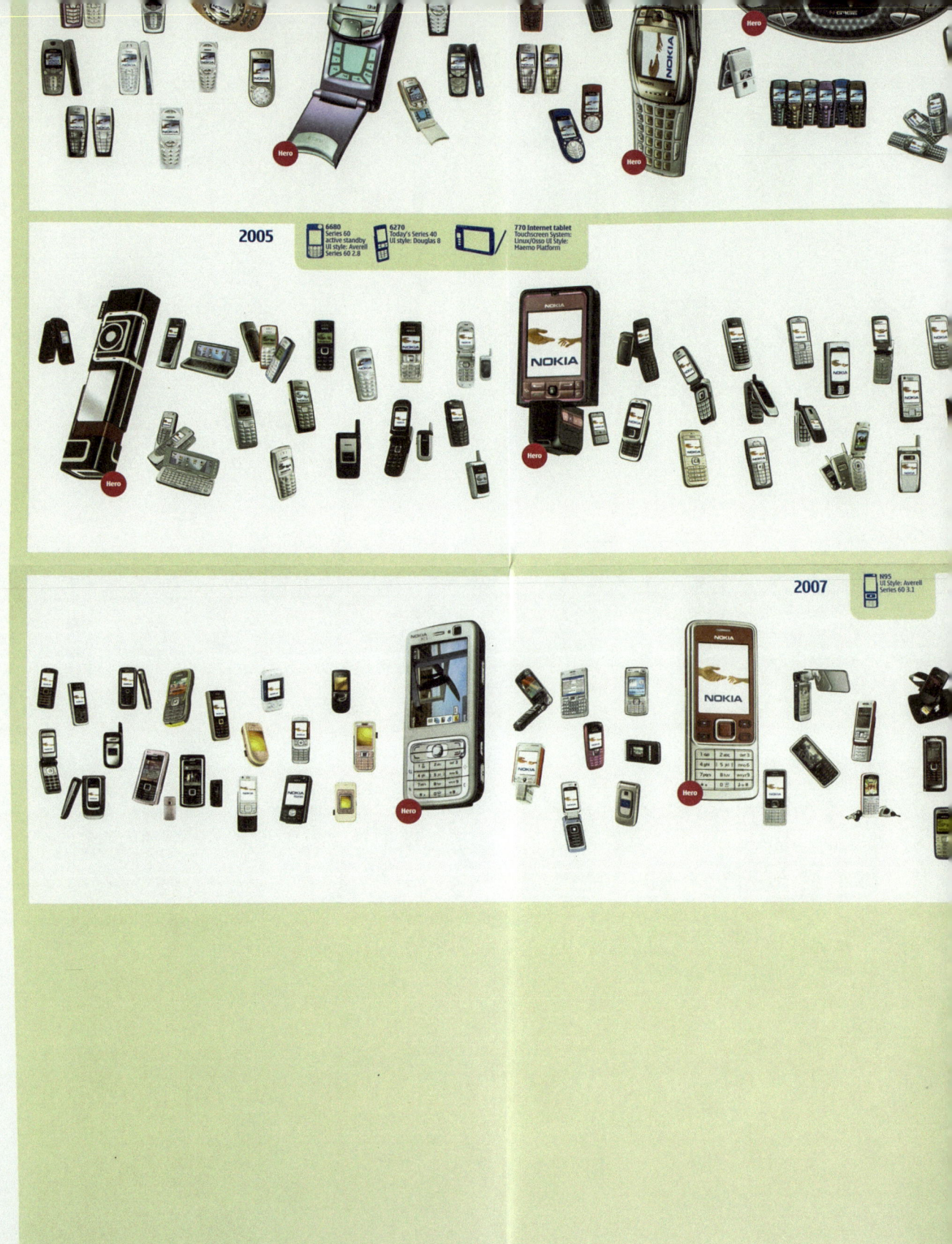

This and previous page
A poster showing phones made between 1982 and 2007 is an insight into Nokia's design past. Now-iconic designs were created during this period of intense evolution which secured Nokia's position as a technological, communications and product design innovator.

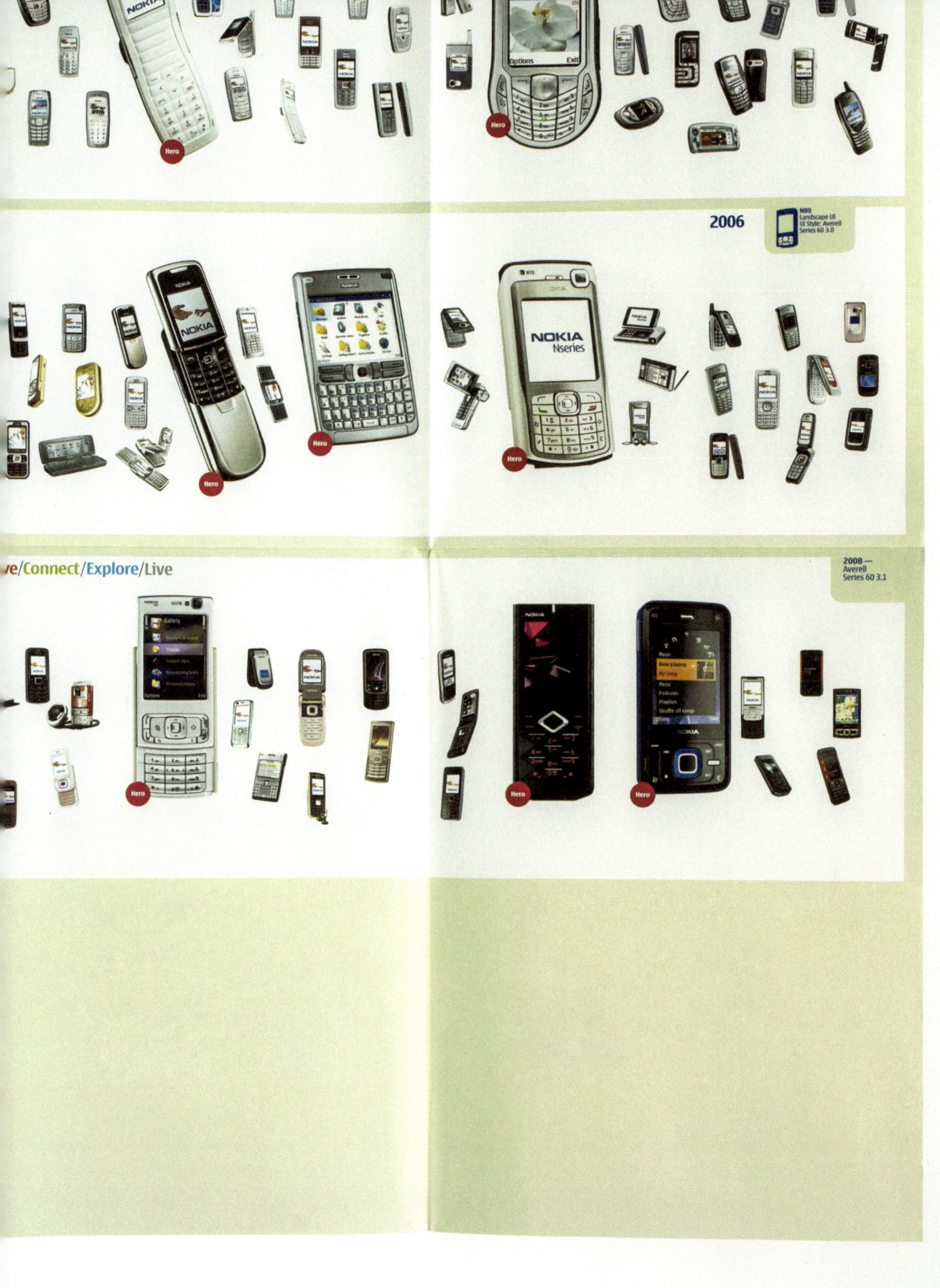

The old adage that Finnish design is inspired by nature is an over-simplification, not to mention an irritation to many designers. But there is truth in the notion too. Finnish culture, not just design, is a product of a social history which in turn has been created by a very specific geography.

Endurance and a strong sense of community are national characteristics formed by Finland's tough climate and landscape. An evolved craft sensibility is a residual consequence of the potent historic need to make tools to survive.

That the Finns are practically-minded, resourceful and skilled at using and appreciating the natural materials around them has everything to do with history and geography. As does their romantic relationship with summer, light and colour.

With Sweden to the West and Russia to the East, Finland's design language is a unique combination of Scandinavian reserve and rich Slavic decoration. Place, with all its many connotations, remains an important creative trigger for young designers and creatives in the region.

COMMUNITY AND PLACE

Sauna is a defining part of Finnish life which has been practised for some two millennia. One of the sauna's strongest characteristics has always been its simplicity, both as ritual and as architecture. Wood, fire, water and air are all that is needed. The log-walled construction, near water and close to nature, has remained largely unchallenged throughout its history.

Sauna is often likened to a church in Finland. It is similarly revered and has its own rituals and respected traditions. As well as being a near-spiritual experience, the communal aspect of sauna is considered important. There are estimated to be some 2 million saunas in Finland today. Building new ones, and preserving old ones, is a constant task.

THE ESSENTIAL RITUAL SAUNA

The simple bathing ritual of sauna is an ever-present custom that is at the centre of Finnish life. The sauna gained popularity over 2,000 years ago and it was the combination of a hard, physical lifestyle and the plentiful supply of wood that originally made this bathing method an efficient process for the rural Finns. From the outset though, sauna has always been more than its sum of parts. As the most sanitised area, the sauna was where children were born, ill people treated and meats cured. Superstitions and folklorish tales have also long existed around the sauna too: that evil spirits could be driven out by the heat was one such belief. Spirituality is often mentioned too: the cleansing of mind as well as body and the contemplative and restorative effects of sauna are valued.

Sauna has been a communal occasion from the beginning. It simply made economical sense for everyone in a home or farm to make use of the sauna once it was heated. As urbanisation spread, so did the social sauna: saunas were built for the factory workers, apartment dwellers and businesses. Most recently, small private saunas have gained popularity and most Finns now have their own. However, the loss of the communal element of this enduring ritual has been noted and is being addressed. The Kulttuurisauna is a popular public sauna in Helsinki designed and run by NOW architects. Meanwhile, the simple, primitive, architectural premise of the sauna; democratic, functional and essential, offers endless attraction for young architects and designers who continue to reinvent and explore it in their work.

This page and following pages
The Rajaportin Sauna was built at the beginning of the 20th century. It the oldest public sauna in Finland and continues to function, day to day, as it always has.

KOE SMOKE SAUNA BY AALTO UNIVERSITY WOOD PROGRAM

Wooden construction defines Finnish architecture. From the first simple log buildings to the latest architectural expressions, wood is the natural material of choice. Its economy, flexibility and efficiency have never been challenged. Traditional log buildings are characterised by their simplicity and clarity. The technique of laying logs horizontally on top of each other produces rectangular, cubic forms. Such primitiveness is still valued, but today wood is used in a more expressive way. At the forefront of exploring and promoting wooden architecture is the Aalto University Wood Program.

This intensive course concludes with the construction of a wood building. In 2012, this was the Koe Smoke Sauna: a modular construction, with prefabricated panels erected on site. Note the external stepped seating area, a generous space that emphasises the communal ritual of sitting outside after bathing, to socialise and enjoy the view.

The Koe Smoke Sauna is a collaborative effort: students both designed and built it as a group. It was erected on the island of Muuratsalo, which, fittingly, is the location for Alvar Aalto's experimental summer house.

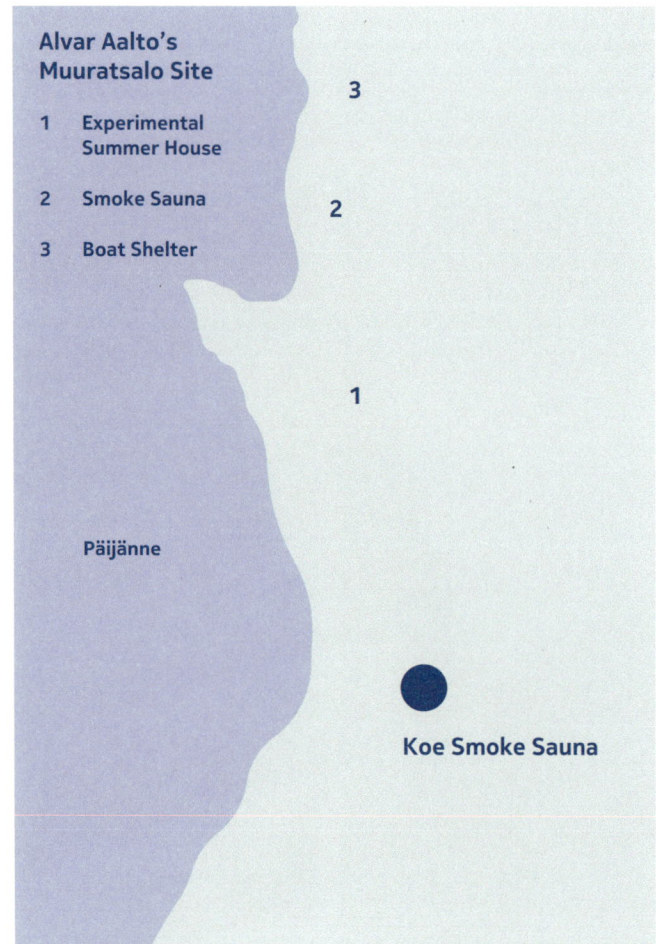

Alvar Aalto's Muuratsalo Site

1 Experimental Summer House
2 Smoke Sauna
3 Boat Shelter

Päijänne

Koe Smoke Sauna

Talkoot is a practice begun in a time when remote Finnish communities had little option but to pull together to get things done.It is a kind of unofficial neighbourhood maintenance and, like much in Finland, is a stoic response to the changing seasons. Today, it remains a popular event that happens across the country twice a year.

At a talkoot, members of a community come together to tidy their little patch of the world in preparation either for the coming winter months or for the much-celebrated summertime. Autumn talkoots typically feature much raking up of leaves, while summer gatherings tend to involve painting, clearing rubbish and general beautifying.

ALL TOGETHER NOW
TALKOOT

Talkoot has its own etiquette to be observed. Notes are posted around the community, which today is increasingly likely to be an apartment block, telling people where and when to meet. When the Talkoot morning comes, tasks are divided among the group. Participants bring food and drink, and after the various jobs are completed everyone will gather to eat, drink and socialise.

There is a solidly practical level to the talkoot ritual, but the reason it is cherished and preserved is as much about the sense of community it engenders. Many Finns remember their first talkoot fondly: teenagers are treated as adults, children are given their own tasks alongside the grown-ups and everyone, regardless of age or background, muddles in together for the greater good. Talkoot reminds Finns of the value of working together, of practical knowledge and skills, and that same sense of community is then wielded in many other areas of Finnish culture to great effect.

These pages and following
The talkoot illustrated here takes place in Suvikumpu, a neighbourhood of architectural note in Tapiola, on the southern coast of Finland. Designed by Raili and Reima Pietilä in 1962, this cluster of buildings is influenced by a Nordic vernacular as well as a modernist ideology. The natural landscape was a large consideration in the situation of the housing blocks and public buildings.

Antto Melasniemi is a highly innovative chef who is interested in the concept of dining, not just cooking. He was behind the Hel Yes! pop-up phenomenon in London and Stockholm. He also has four restaurants in Helsinki that each combine a no-fuss approach to dining with the finest ingredients Finland has to offer.

'It's interesting to rethink the whole restaurant concept,' he says. A former student of International Design Business Management at Aalto University and formerly the keyboard player for rock band HIM, he now loves to collaborate with designers who are not afraid to take risks. The eclectic results include projects such as the Trojan Bar, bar hidden in a wooden box.

EXTRA-SENSORY PERCEPTION
ANTTO MELASNIEMI

How did you get into the restaurant business?
I started out playing music, but at some point I became interested in cooking and so trained as a chef. Then I went to work abroad in London and France for a while. In 2004, I returned to Finland and the next year I started my first restaurant, Kuurna, with Heikki Purhonen. I've always been more interested in restaurants as a whole, not just the food. That's why I started working with designers.

Now I'm mostly doing concept design. I took a course in International Design Business Management at the Aalto University. I'm in charge of the Kellohalli restaurant and events in the Abattoir area, which is a new food culture hub in Helsinki. My latest project was a lot smaller, though. I got this idea of a kind of a parasite bar, tossed it into the air, and my friend made a prototype of the Trojan Bar, which is a bar hidden inside a box. You can wheel this wooden box into your friend's restaurant like a Trojan horse, open it and turn it into a bar, and start selling booze and take your friend's business away.

What do you look for in potential collaborators?
I'm more of a manager than a designer, since I depend on the input of professional designers. I concentrate on being the team leader. It's interesting to hear what a graphic designer or an architect thinks of food. I want everyone to contribute to everything. I appreciate the ability to take risks and to step outside the comfort zone, which is a surprisingly rare thing.

Tell us about how you like to work.
My way of working involves a lot of doing and sometimes not much thinking—just trying things out and then doing them over if necessary. I like to make quick decisions, since you can always reconsider if they don't work. I'm rarely happy with the first version of anything, which might be a bit frustrating at times. I'm a bit chaotic to work with, so it's a good thing I have a lot of organised people around me.

Tell me about the Hel Yes! pop-up restaurant project. How did it develop from an idea into reality?
I was doing a lot of events and festivals abroad related to design and culture, but what annoyed me was the way they were always very sporadic—and the masses of people were just overwhelming. So I came up with the idea of a temporary restaurant that would be a bit more intimate; a more social experience. The idea for Hel Yes! was born, which was a pop-up restaurant in collaboration with the Finnish Cultural Institute in London. I asked designer Klaus Haapaniemi along and together we invited a bunch of other people to collaborate.

We chose London as the venue, since people there are very open-minded when it comes to trying new things. We chose a mythical pagan forest theme, which was represented by rabbits and other animals in the decor. It was all about hunting and gathering. We did a second Hel Yes! in Stockholm, which was very different. We collaborated with choreographer Kenneth Kvarnström and that was about movement. Both projects taught me a lot about directing teams of strong, creative people.

What do you think about the relationship between food and design?
Traditionally, design has been present in food through tableware. Industrial design is historically a fairly recent development, since engineering and craftsmanship have been around for a much longer time. It's the same with food. The field is dominated by two extremes: industrial production and so-called gourmet dining with a strong emphasis on handiwork. Maybe we could think of a new way of producing food that's somewhere between the two?

Can food change society?
Definitely. Food is already a strong political force, especially where there's a shortage of it. Lately, the music business has had to come up with an entirely new business logic. It's interesting to rethink the whole concept of the restaurant. Could there be a more innovative way to do it? What about offering everyone free food? It's definitely a future challenge for us all.

What turns food into an experience?
Stories and hospitality are important. It has to be more than just basic service. We talk about food too much when we should concentrate on the whole feeling. Everything around you contributes to the experience: the space, all the sounds or music there, what it feels like to sit down. Ideally, it should actually be impossible to determine everything that goes into it.

Where do you go for creative inspiration?
Deep in the forest there's a mailbox with no name on it that's full of great ideas. Not really! I'm just a bit impatient and always interested in new things. The best way to create is to empty your head, which I try to do by skiing, or swimming, or taking a walk in the forest.

How does your nationality affect your work?
My roots have a big influence on what I do. A certain stubbornness and stamina are considered pretty Finnish. One just goes through with things, no matter what happens. There's also a good kind of laziness in the Finnish way of working: we try to get our work done in the most sensible way possible, meaning it requires the least amount of effort. There's an unassuming determination in us Finns that gets things done.

I'm also inspired by the natural forms of Finnish ingredients. I like to figure out ways to cook food that don't involve manipulating the ingredients too much. I'm not big on dicing things up into pretty cubes. I love to just stick carrots in a vat of something and leave them there for a couple of days.

What would you like to say to people about Finnish food culture?
We're only just starting to build up this new-found pride and confidence about our food. It's still pretty common to think of food as just fuel here. The value of sensory pleasure is under-appreciated. But we have a short, intense growth period, so our ingredients have extremely strong flavours. Gathering wild herbs and vegetables is easy, since there's a lot of wilderness everywhere.

We don't have direct access to an ocean, so we don't have real seafood. The scope of ingredients is limited in a way, but I see that as an interesting challenge. Compared to other Scandinavian countries, we have a lot of eastern influences in our cuisine. There's also a good primitive vibe: our entire culture has a rough edge that hasn't been spoiled by too much civilization.

I'm always been more interested in restaurants as a whole, not just the food there. That's why I started working with designers.

ANTTO MELASNIEMI

Previous and this page
Melasniemi's Solar Kitchen project was a collaboration with Spanish designer Martí Guixé who designed metal ovens that harnessed the heat of the sun to cook. Melasniemi toured Europe with the concept in the summer of 2011 before setting up a temporary kitchen in Helsinki, pictured here.

ANTTO MELASNIEMI

MARTÍ GUIXÉ

2011 HELSINKI

It might seem a gamble to develop a restaurant concept where sunshine is the only power source, but Melasniemi limited the risk by only opening on sunny days. Salad was on standby.

LAPIN KULTA SOLAR KITCHEN RESTAURANT

OPENING DAYS: SUNNY DAYS

The best way to create is to empty your head, which I try to do by skiing or swimming, or taking a walk in the forest.

ANTTO MELASNIEMI

This page and following pages
When not in one of his many kitchens or working on new and exciting dining concepts, Antto Melasniemi might be found in the wilds of the Finnish countryside. Ingredients that can be found locally and seasonally have long inspired his cooking. Here, Melasniemi forages for mushrooms in the same woods he has been coming to for many years and cooks them in the open with a leg of Finnish lamb.

In 2009, photographer Paavo Lehtonen shot a series of pictures in and around Helsinki. Titled Local Shops, its subject was the dying breed of small, independent stores and their owners, which are slowly being pushed out of the city by the arrival of large supermarkets. 'I wanted to highlight local shops and traditional trades,' says Lehtonen. 'Little shops that people have put their whole life into.

I wanted to highlight the personal paths of these vendors and their pride in owning and running a small local business.'
These stores are the last bastions of some traditional trades, as well as being centres for local communities.

COMMUNITY AND COMMERCE
PAAVO LEHTONEN

Previous pages
Markku Väisänen's shoe repair shop on Vaasankatu.

Selma Palmu, textile shop on Neljäs linja.

Top left
Sandwich shop on Pursimiehenkatu.

Bottom left
Elintarvike Heinonen, grocery shop on Museokatu.

Above
Antiikkiliike Kotikadun Mainio Wanhatavara, antique shop on Eteläinen Hesperiankatu.

A disused rail yard in Helsinki's Pasila area has been transformed into an urban farm, public space, café and place of learning by environmental NGO Dodo. The project is a demonstration of how Helsinki's younger generation reacts to the problems of urbanisation, a relatively new dilemma in Finland.

The Turntable Urban Garden project has openness, community, and green living at its core—the traditional Finnish values translate well into contemporary environmental activism, it seems. The Turntable Urban Garden has turned a city wasteland into a popular destination and is a flagship for urban regeneration, Finnish style.

GROWING STRONG
TURNTABLE URBAN GARDEN

Helsinki is a growing city with an expanding population; urbanisation has moved fast here in recent years. Dodo is the most prolific of several Helsinki groups that are concerned with the 'everyday sustainability' of the city. Coming up with new ways of living, moving and consuming is their purpose.

The Turntable Urban Garden project began in 2009 when the group (led by Jaska Lehtonen, Kirmo Kivelä, Päivi Raivio and Joseph Mulcahy) took over this disused railway site with the ambition of turning the space into an urban farm. In 2012, with the backing of Helsinki Design Capital, the project expanded. A greenhouse-cum-café was built and the area became the hub of Dodo's activities: 'an urban farming test lab and a source for learning and inspiration.' The food grown on site is served in the café, and workshops and events are a constant draw.

Finnish culture is so closely aligned with nature that dealing with a lack of green urban space or unsustainability might seem an unnecessary concern. Yet the reality of a changing landscape and evolving population are real and groups like Dodo therefore have a substantial part to play in awareness and action. Interestingly, the communal workshops, activities and work-parties (talkoots) that are part of Dodo's combative approach are familiar tools with a distinctively Finnish tone.

Right and below
In the summer, visitors to the Turntable café enjoy meals made from the produce that is grown around them.

Following page
The greehouse and surrounding garden were built using recycled materials.

Established in 2004, Avanto Architects might be a young practice, but it already has several celebrated buildings under its belt and more substantial projects on the drawing board. Avanto's co-founders Anu Puustinen and Ville Hara are particularly concerned with the social aspect of architecture.

A prime example is their approach to the communal sauna, inventing new architectural solutions for the time-honoured ritual. They are also focused on reintroducing traditional systems into their work and building in wood is, they say, just second nature.

GOOD CLEAN ARCHITECTURE
AVANTO ARCHITECTS

What is it like to be an architect in Finland at the moment? Is it an optimistic time?
Ville Hara: There's a young generation coming up and growing now. A lot of our classmates have won very large competitions for big public buildings. So it is very interesting at the moment.

Is the architecture scene small?
VH: Yes. And everybody knows each other.

Why are things good?
VH: Economically it's very tough. But there is a culture of competition here. Whenever there is a major public building to be built, there is an open competition and anybody can participate. Even my grandmother could participate—although she's not an architect.

And why is that good?
VH: It is very good because winning is about the quality of the work, not about the personality of the architect. So in our culture it is not so much about big name architects like Foster, although his work is good. It is not so centralised here: anybody has the chance of getting work. New practices are popping up all the time.

Anu Puustinen: It's very equal for the newcomers.

I suppose that's a great way for young practices to get the experience that they need to progress?
AP: That's true. That's how we started as well.

Which was the project that you began with?
AP: We started the office in 2004 after winning the competition for the Chapel of St. Lawrence. There were something like 200 entries for that. But even before that Ville had realised a fantastic project for the Helsinki Zoo.

Is 200 a normal amount of entries?
AP: Sometimes it's more than 500 entries. In the past, the competition was mostly for Finnish architects, but nowadays all European countries can participate. Actually, most of our professors from the Helsinki University of Technology participated for the Chapel of St. Lawrence competition. We were really surprised to win that: it was quite a small project, but very challenging.

And what made your entry the winning one?
AP: We might say that it was because it was very respectful towards the site, which was a medieval church and cemetery: 1,000 square metres, more or less, on top of the ground and spaces also underground.

VH: It took eight years to complete. So when we won the competition, everyone said: 'How are these children going to be able to build anything?' And when we were ready with the building we were already middle-aged.

Are those kind of competitions normally won by young practices?
AP: Not always, no.

VH: These competitions also give the possibility for the older generation to renew their careers. In this building we have one very famous office where there is an older professor who must be 70 years old. And he is always inventing new things and creating very fresh architecture.

Is infrastructure building still important in Helsinki? Is there still a demand for new housing, for example?
VH: After the Second World War there were national programmes to arrange a home for everybody. But also after that our structure changed quite a lot to become more urban. Finland had for a long time been a very rural and agricultural country. Nowadays a lot of people are still moving from the countryside to the cities. There is a growing urbanisation even now, though the population in Finland doesn't really grow. A lot of new housing is being built in Helsinki: old industrial areas are being turned into housing and there are several developments.

And are you involved in any of those?
AP: We do a lot of city planning for the cities of Espoo and Helsinki. We can be dealing with big structures that will be visible in 20 or 30 years.

It must be interesting to think on that scale…
VH: What is interesting for us has been to work on very different scales. We have been doing product design on a very, very small scale and then also urban design which is the biggest scale—and everything in between. It is very diverse.

AP: I really enjoy it. We don't want to select just one area or to specialise. We have done some gardening products, for example. And then we have also done some work together with UPM [a Finnish pulp, paper and timber company], which has not been realised yet.

VH: The Garden Shed is a kind of combination of a storage and greenhouse. Linda Bergroth was the designer that participated in the project. She made one into her own country cottage: very minimal!

What else are you currently building?
AP: Right now it's quite difficult to build anything in Finland. But we have done several one-family housing projects and some product design also for the housing estate companies: small houses. The Dice House is one sketch that we've done for a housing company. The project was started by the Finnish Cultural Foundation. They wanted to have a totally wooden house that uses zero energy and has no machine ventilation. And that's quite uncommon nowadays in Finland. New houses are not made that way.

Is it a modern version of the veterans' houses?
AP: Yes, that was the brief that we got: it should be something like the veterans' houses used to be, but for people living nowadays. It is completely wooden and not very big: it is 120 square metres. A family with three children can live there, and there are two greenhouses attached to the house already.

It's perhaps ironic that the project Ville Hara is best known for is a shed. Although humble, the project for Kekkilä is a good rendition, albeit in microcosm, of the principles he holds dear: Garden Shed is a modular construction, ecologically built and thoughtfully designed. He collaborated with designer Linda Bergroth on the project and the version pictured is her interpretation of the shed as summer house.

Is the inclusion of nature important to you? Or important as a theme?
AP: We want to bring it into every project, but we are rarely asked to do that.

VH: Buildings in Finland often have some kind of views to nature and this kind of thing is like the border between the inside and outside. It is an interesting theme.

AP: These greenhouses are working as in-between spaces, between the garden and the house, because we have such a long winter here. We need this buffer if we want to grow something.

VH: This project is also related to a discussion about saving energy and building green. How to do it? There are two views. There's the engineering school that says you have to make houses that are sealed, like plastic bags. And then there is another school that says that you can have breathing structures and air-conditioning without machines: building in a traditional way. It's funny. It's seen as an innovative approach, even though it's traditional.

What else are you working on?
AP: We are doing some invitation competitions right now. And open competitions as well. We have done several saunas during the last few years too. First, we made a kind of product design and then a log sauna called Kyly. This is a very traditional way of building saunas here but we used it in a modern way. It's a new concept. It is a composition which is built around the ritual of going to sauna and purifying yourself, mentally and physically.

So the ritual informed the design concept?
AP: We have been laughing that it's a little bit similar to the chapel. I see a lot of sauna projects and a lot of chapel projects and they are interchangeable to a certain degree.

They are both important building types. Are they used in a similar way?
AP: Yes. Sauna is a kind of ritual that makes you feel good and you need a temple for that!

VH: For Finns, the sauna is almost like a holy place. It used to be the place where you would give birth, because it is the cleanest place. A long time ago, of course. And also where someone who had died was kept before being interred. So even though it is an everyday thing—people do sauna quite a lot even today—it's still a place that people respect. There are some people who think you shouldn't shout or be noisy in a sauna. It's still a kind of holy place.

AP: We wanted to make our design from logs in as simple a way as possible. We thought about the functions and the relations of functions and also used the floor level as a part of the composition. So you first take two steps away from everyday life to get into this area where you can change your clothes. You can sit down and start to relax and get rid of everyday stress.

VH: It was built for a fair and it has no joints, so you can reuse all the materials.

A new Cultural Sauna opened in Helsinki recently. Is sauna still just as important as it used to be in Finnish culture?
AP: Yes.

VH: You know, there is this tradition that all the decision-making in Finland is done inside sauna.

VH: There's a cultural change. It used to be the case that apartments or flats didn't have any saunas, so you had to go to public saunas. Some of them still survive. We are actually also designing one at the seaside and there's a couple more coming. We take advantage of the fact that Helsinki has some points where you have a direct sea view: you can see all the way to Tallinn. It's totally open.

AP: Next time you come it will hopefully be built…

So that is the sauna situation. What of the many wooden church buildings? To an outsider it would seem that Finland is especially religious. Is it?
VH: That's a good question. A lot of people have been thinking about that because the power of the church has got somehow diminished in many ways and society is not so religious anymore. But it is probably because people are moving from the countryside to the city centres: there are new housing districts and it is a kind of a tradition that every one has to have a church. So still today there are new churches being built.

AP: And when a church is built using tax money, there is a responsibility to make it durable, so the churches should last at least 200 years.

And what about wood construction? You use it. Others still use it a lot too. Is that something that you enjoy, working with wood and using it as a material?
VH: Mmm. It's kind of funny because for foreigners it's always something they think is special in Finland, this wood construction. But for us, it's not that special because it's a very traditional material and it's very natural to use it. It's easy to work the material; it's very cheap also, which is always an advantage. And, of course, it's pleasant to look at, it ecological—it has all sorts of advantages. We don't really think about it.

AP: Sometimes we use wood and then when something else is needed, we use something else.

VH: There's no special ideology about it.

What are your ambitions for the practice?
AP: It's a difficult question. We don't think about whether we want to do housing or not. It's rather that we think: what can we learn about? Because, I think, now we have done this for 10 years, we are at the point where we want to learn something.

VH: We want new challenges. One new challenge we have is the sector of well-being and health.

VH: And care buildings. We won a competition for a building for people with autism spectrum disorders. For us it's important to put yourself in the client's role: to empathise and put yourself in their situation. And we believe that this is how you get good architecture for people. Not so that we make some kind of sculpture or become 'star architects', but to have more of a human approach in a way.

AP: It feels good to have a social aspect to everything we do.

Previous and this page Each arm of the Four-Cornered Villa reaches out to a different vista. The still, contemplative and light interior is in contrast to the dark exterior. The simple house is built for a simple lifestyle: it has no running water or electricity, is heated by wood and is in a remote area by Lake Vaskivesi.

The Finnish education constantly ranks high is international comparative studies. The system that delivers these results is unique and innovative, and the challenge for Finland's architects has been to propel it forward in the design of intelligent, smart school buildings.

Verstas Architects' have applied such a fresh approach to educational architecture that their Saunalahati school in Espoo is being coined a 'future school'. The successful way in which the principles of Finnish education are supported and met in architectural form means that this building is being used as a blueprint, at home and abroad, for new school building.

AN EDUCATION
SAUNALAHTI SCHOOL

Verstas Architects met the brief for a 10,000-square-metre building to house 750 pupils, a day-care centre, a preschool, classrooms for 1 to 9 year olds and a youth house with their design that supported the forward-thinking programme of education in every small detail.

The school is a multi-purpose building intended for use by the local community too, therefore Verstas gave the building an open character and made it face the new residential area of Saunalahti. Importantly, each interior and exterior space is a potential place for learning—the usual conflict of classroom versus public space does not apply here. To that end, flexible and communal spaces such as a large plaza and amphitheatre-like space outside and a multi-functional hall at the heart of the building are given prominence. And there are spaces to meet or learn or play with different scales and atmospheres throughout the building. An undulating copper roof links the different areas of the structure together. Throughout, the palette of materials used is natural and high quality. Even the positioning of schoolyards was carefully considered; the younger children's school day is short so their schoolyard gets the most sunshine in the morning, while the older children, who enjoy a longer day's education, are positioned so as to reap the benefits of the afternoon sun.

Finnish children do not face mandatory testing until the end of their final year at secondary school. A uniform quality of education is maintained across schools with teachers being employed from the top percentage of university graduates and the differences between the weakest and strongest students are the smallest in the world. Architecture and design, as so succinctly demonstrated at the Saunalahati school, is playing an increasingly important role in maintaining the quality of Finland's educational system.

The different environments in the school encourage interaction. The organisation of the spaces can be compared to urban design; just like in a city there are public, semi-public and private areas.

Principles of equality are firmly upheld in Finnish society, from attitudes towards gender—Finland has elected two female presidents in the last 15 years—to the architecture tendering process, which allows everyone to apply for even major projects. Such principles are an important consideration for Finland's makers.

Characters like Kaj Franck and Alvar Aalto led the way when it came to putting social concerns at the forefront of creative practices. They worked at a time when design was widely seen as a tool for change. Society was modernising quickly and design was needed to enable objects and buildings to solve urgent problems. Democratic design meant producing honest, everyday, hard-working objects and creating spaces that were accessible and beneficial to all.

Today, the icons of Finnish design are more likely to be found in a suburban living room than a museum. And good Finnish design remains democratic, with many young designers still speaking about their social conscience and their desire to make accessible, everyday design.

DEMOCRATIC DESIGN

Oiva Toikka once described Kaj Franck as 'king of the hill'. Franck was a natural leader. During his long and fruitful career, he achieved some remarkable goals and has inspired generations of designers to marry a social conscience with their work. Dedicated, passionate and talented, Franck will forever be remembered for his years at Arabia and Iittala and respected for his position at the epicentre of Finnish design culture.

Päivi Jantunen is an expert on Franck, and was a colleague too. 'Glass has been my world since 1973,' she says. Päivi worked in communications and marketing at Iittala, in London and at Nuutajärvi. She has had the opportunity to work with such personalities as Franck, Oiva Toikka and Harri Koskinen. She was asked to write a book about Franck, called Kaj & Franck, to celebrate the hundredth anniversary of his birth. Here she answers our questions about him.

KING OF THE HILL
KAJ FRANCK

What was Kaj Franck's mission when he was appointed art director at Arabia?
Kaj Franck was employed by Arabia in 1945. A separate department for the development of household products in serial production was established the same year. Kaj was appointed the director of that new area. This new department separated art production from products for the table. Arabia had accumulated an enormous assortment of fine dinnerware series and separate anonymous household items over the years.

Kaj wanted a revolution in product categories to match the new post-war situation. There was a great need for household goods in smaller and more urban homes, both for middle-class and working-class families—and there were more working women too. All these changes in the Finnish home called for a new generation of household goods. Creating them was Kaj Franck's mission.

Was the Kilta collection Franck's first true articulation of his style? What were its basic principles?
Kilta was the first complete concept to respond to 'modern needs'. He went to the extreme and cut down the initial number of pieces to eight items, each of which could be used in a multitude of ways. The strict and practical Kilta was also easy to mix and match with goods already in homes. This mixing and matching also made it possible to dress Kilta equally well for festive occasions and everyday use. It was produced in a small range of well thought out colours. No decoration was one of Kaj's visual principles.

How were Franck's modern designs for Arabia first received by the public?
The launch of Kilta was backed up by a vigorous collaboration with women's organisations, such as the Martha organisation, with the help of the information department of Arabia. Even Kaj himself met the public to demonstrate the 'new way'. In my opinion, Kilta became most popular with middle-class homes. People collected parts of Kilta little by little. They were also given as gifts. That was very different from the pompous wedding present dinnerware tradition that lived on until rather recently in many countries. Perhaps to renew the tableware was one of the easiest ways to express modern living.

Did Franck feel a social responsibility?
Kaj had a very strong social conscience which had developed during his years in the army during the war. He hated all kind of boasting in words and in deeds in all aspects of life. Kilta was nothing superficial for Kaj. It was a real expression of his social responsibility.

The principles of teamwork were important to Franck. Can you tell me a bit about this?
My personal experiences of Kaj Franck are from the glass works at Nuutajärvi. But I am sure that the same applies to his team workers at Arabia and, as I have heard, also at the university as a teacher. Kaj appreciated skilled craftsmen. He was always most considerate with the glass-makers. He never sat while he was working with the team on the shop floor.

The importance of teamwork was also expressed by the principal of anonymity regarding serial production. A mass-produced piece was always a result of teamwork, for good and for bad. Therefore Kaj did not think production pieces should be signed by any one person. The process involved people from production, marketing and design, even the economy department. Art pieces, particularly unique pieces, were a totally different story. He gladly signed his unique pieces—those he accepted as first class.

How hands-on was Franck? Did he enjoy the actual making of the pieces?
Kaj was an interior designer by education. He did not work on the materials himself. But he made those wonderful small drawings on postcard-sized pieces of cardboard with written instructions! He would send them to the mould-makers, the master blower and others in advance for consultation. He was very familiar with the materials and techniques, even the skills of individual workers and could make perfect use of this knowledge.

How did Franck reconcile his mass-production work with making art pieces? Did he work differently on each or place a different emphasis on them?
Mass production is always very cost-driven. Even if you started with something totally new, which you didn't know everything about, the aim was always to make a series at a reasonable cost. But making unique pieces was a free, experimental and aesthetic opportunity, and a holiday from costs, at least within the boundaries of the few hours of expensive group work devoted to this purpose.

Kaj believed that this free experimentation and artistic work could also produce ideas for mass production. But this high-class art production was also a feather in the hat for the rest of the brand. It was also a great opportunity for the working team. For all of us. The emphasis was certainly on mass production. But one would think that it was also invigorating for Kaj to work independently for a moment in art production. But mass production of good design was surely closest to his social conscience.

The original Kilta collection was later streamlined and renamed Teema. The popular collection is still sold today.

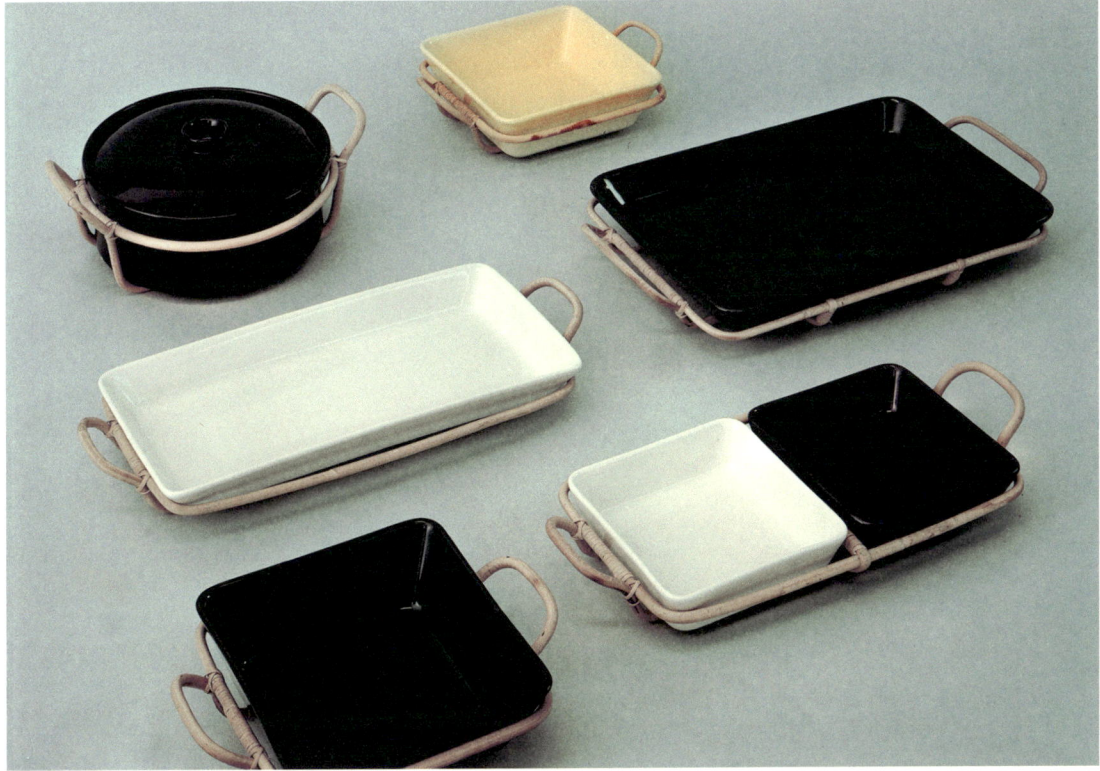

What were the key innovations Franck brought to design and the production process?

I think that most important was the drastic reduction of the number of different items. The same few pieces could be used by very different households. Getting rid of the aristocratic-based dinnerware thinking and replacing it with shapes that suited modern living and modern industrial production resulted in economical yet aesthetic products.

Kaj was also an early ecologist. This aspect is in harmony with his belief in fewer, long-lasting products which do not require excessive space. Kaj did not only apply his principles in his own design, he also influenced generations of younger colleagues, and his students too. And perhaps his use of colour—strong colours without decoration—was new at the time. He created the wonderful colour scheme for glass which is still very important for Iittala.

How important was Franck as a teacher?

Generations of design students of all different departments of the University of Art and Design in Helsinki [now part of Aalto University] have enjoyed Kaj as a teacher. He was a very innovative and demanding teacher with very hands-on projects. The importance of ecology hardly escaped his students. Kaj was also invited to several countries to discuss their national design policies and lecture at their design schools, including Japan and Ireland.

What was Franck's character like? For someone so closely aligned with utility, might you think him austere?

Kaj was generally very well behaved. Perhaps he was a little distant. He was a rather small man with great authority. He was not afraid to fight for his cause with anyone. But he was also a lot of fun. Very witty. And he had a most refined aesthetic touch: he would draw attention to modest but beautiful objects. He also appreciated beautiful handicraft. It is well known that he was fond of Japanese aesthetics. His early film footage from his trips to America and Japan show his sharp observations of people and phenomenons and a great sense of humour.

He was very articulate. He was perhaps at this best when chatting and discussing with his colleague, Professor Oiva Toikka. Both were masters of words. Not big theory or pomp, but very lively and funny. Kaj lived in a small apartment in the same house with the Toikka family and always sat at their dinner table while he was at Nuutajärvi. Two great masters in very everyday situations, often watching TV after the meal. Nothing very special; still always special.

Kaj was very fond of flowers and made several gardens. At his Nuutajärvi home he had planted a cyclamen by a rock. I never saw it bloom but it survived many winters. It was typical Kaj to choose such a small and delicate plant.

DEMOCRATIC DESIGN

Kaj was also an early ecologist. This aspect is in harmony with his belief in fewer, long-lasting products which do not require excessive space.

PÄIVI JANTUNEN

Above
Teema 1952.

Left
Kaj Franck was an enthusiastic professor at the University of Art and Design, another example of the legacy he has passed on to generations of Finnish designers.

DEMOCRATIC DESIGN

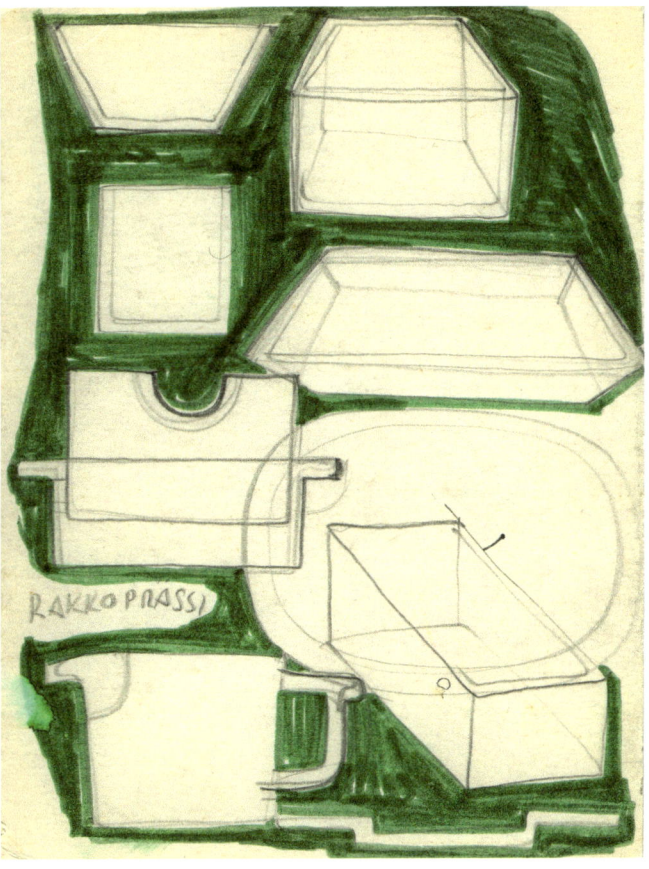

Left
Saippuakupla (Soap Bubble) vases, 1951–61.

Above
Franck's simple illustrative sketches belie the sophistication of his work.

Top left
Kartio glasses
1958.

Top right
Kremlin Bells decanters
1955–68.

DEMOCRATIC DESIGN

Of all Finland's makers, Tapio Wirkkala is perhaps the most prolific. He worked first as a sculptor, then as a graphic and industrial designer, and counts plastic ketchup bottles, metalware, banknotes, mass-produced furniture and a Finlandia vodka bottle among his work.

Wirkkala lent his techniques and academic abilities to the Finnish design scene but his greatest gift was the poetic 'Finnishness' that he imbued his designs with. It made his work a great national export. And when we talk about the close connection between nature and Finnish design, it is perhaps his works that we have in mind.

A NATURAL DESIGNER
TAPIO WIRKKALA

TAPIO WIRKKALA

Tapio Wirkkala was born in Hanko, in the south of Finland, and studied ornamental sculpting at the Central School of Arts and Crafts. He had a deep respect for materials and abided by his ethos that 'all materials have their own unwritten laws… You should never be violent with a material you're working on, and the designer should aim at being in harmony with his material.' This referred to the banal and everyday as much as the precious. His leaf-shaped dishes, cut from plywood and hollowed to create a striped effect, exploit the layered properties of a material usually associated with cheap mass-produced goods. It is one of his most iconic designs.

It is, however, his poetic forms that drew the affection of the nation. He says he was greatly influenced by the natural environment of his native land, particularly Lapland, as pieces such as his Iceberg vase attest.

Forms ingrained in his psyche—leaves, flower calyces and mushrooms, the shapes of birds or fish, ice formations and water droplets—often found their way into his work, whether consciously or not. While his work is always utilitarian and functional, he successfully exerted a spiritual influence on modernist Scandinavian design. The fact that he reinterpreted Finland's environment and its traditional culture for his audience over and over again is key to the affection Finns still hold for him. Famously, he used a Sami knife to carve out forms and designs.

Wirkkala's work was first introduced to the public in 1946, when he entered a competition by Iittala for engraved glass models. He produced the Kanttarelli hand-blown vase, with a flaring rim, and won. Iittala hired him instantly, and between the 1940s and 1980s he designed more than 400 different glass objects and glassware series for the brand.

From 1951 to 1954, he was artistic director of the Central School of Industrial Design in Helsinki. During this time, he won a large number of awards, including three gold medals at the Triennale in Milan in 1951, and three more in 1954. He had a brief collaboration with Raymond Loewy in New York from 1955 to 1956, before returning to Helsinki and setting up in practice. Over his career, he also designed utility objects for Ahlström, Airam and Kultakeskus, glass for Venini in Italy and porcelain for Rosenthal in Germany.

Above and top right
Tapio Wirkkala.

Bottom, left to right
Ultima Thule 1968.

Finlandia Vodka was launched in 1970 and Wirkkala designed the very first bottle. His icy rendition for the local brand became an instant classic. Harri Koskinen has designed the current bottle.

Wirkkala's Bolle bottles 1966–67 for Venini demonstrate a quiet clarity.

DEMOCRATIC DESIGN

All materials have their own unwritten laws.

TAPIO WIRKKALA

Wirkkala used the natural characteristics in any material to great effect. Whether the molten quality of glass, mastered many times to represent ice and water, or the grain of wood, as seen here in the Leaf-Form Platter 1951.

Ask someone outside Finland to name one Finnish designer or architect and they'll probably say Alvar Aalto. He completed hundreds of projects between the 1920s and the 1970s, designing buildings, furniture, lighting, textiles and glassware. He also co-founded Artek. Countless books have been written about his work and life, and many of his designs are still in production today.

Aalto himself was full of character, a fact that many believe was key to his success. Markku Lahti, head of the Alvar Aalto Museum from 1973 to 2010, says: 'Alvar Aalto was a little man, a phrase he frequently used, but when he stepped into the room, there was an aura around him because he had such charisma.' Markku Lahti and Esa Laaksonen, directors of the Alvar Aalto Academy today, tell us what they know about the great man himself.

CHARISMA AND VISION
ALVAR AALTO

Right
Alvar Aalto.

Bottom right
Aalto's Experimental Summer House 1953 was a sketchpad of ideas. Its exterior is a mosaic of different-sized bricks and tiles.

Alvar Aalto was less than 30 years old when he designed his first buildings, but he never really talked about his early work. The project that he was more likely to discuss was the one that made him famous: the Paimio Sanatorium, completed in 1932. It was featured in major architecture magazines all over the world and won acclaim for its clever, functional design. The building, and everything in it, had been designed by Aalto to be entirely utilitarian.

Aalto was less than 30 years old when he designed his first buildings, but he never really talked about his early work. The project that he was more likely to discuss was the one that made him famous: the Paimio Sanatorium, completed in 1932. It was featured in major architecture magazines all over the world and won acclaim for its clever, functional design. The building, and everything in it, had been designed by Aalto to be entirely utilitarian.

It was around the same time that Aalto designed some of his most famous products and furniture, which were exhibited at many international design fairs. Suddenly, Aalto was everywhere. 'He was unusually international, a real cosmopolitan,' says Lahti. 'Aalto was terribly social and good at talking to people. He travelled a lot and met all the important architects around the world. He had his first exhibition at the MoMA in New York in 1938, which was exceptional for a Finnish architect.'

Aalto enjoyed his life and used a lot of his money to travel. 'Aalto wasn't very practical and it was his wives [he was married twice] who took care of the practicalities,' says Lahti. When Aalto married for the first time, he took his new wife Aino Marsio, a talented designer in her own right who also collaborated with her husband, on a trip to Italy that inspired him a lot. 'Aalto always said that it was fine to borrow from other people's work as long as you did it better,' says Lahti. The Italian influence is especially visible in the Työväentalo (Workers' Club) 1928 in Jyväskylä, with its references to Renaissance architecture. In 1928, Aalto travelled to Paris and saw the modernist buildings for the first time. 'That sparked the next big phase in Aalto's work, which stayed with him for the rest of his life,' says Lahti. Aalto remained outward looking throughout his career, While being influenced by the world outside of Finland, he was an influential figure himself.

Esa Laaksonen is director of the Alvar Aalto Academy. He says that part of Aalto's success was the way he collaborated with other people. 'He worked closely with professionals like carpenters and metalsmiths. He also understood people's needs very well.' Aalto wrote a lot about the relationship between the client and the architect. 'If he didn't like someone, he refused to work with them,' says Lahti. When Aalto was friends with the client, it inspired him. 'He always thought about the well-being of that person and built the house around his needs,' says Lahti. Aalto took the same user-focused approach when designing public buildings and always started from within. 'He drew the interior first,' says Lahti. 'After that came the façade because that was the face of the building. The back of the building wasn't that important for him.'

Despite his cosmopolitan credentials, Aalto was proud of his roots. 'When the Winter War between Russia and Finland broke out in 1939, Aalto was at the New York World's Fair,' says Lahti. 'He could have stayed, but he wanted to

> **He always thought about the well-being of that person and built the house around his needs.**
>
> MARKKU LAHTI

DEMOCRATIC DESIGN

come back to Finland.' By then Aalto was in his forties and a major player among the cultural elite. But he wasn't the only one. 'He was alongside other great architects like Viljo Revell and Aarne Ervi,' says Laaksonen. 'Cultural circles were small. Everybody knew each other.'

Aalto remained popular until the 1960s, but then the mood shifted. 'The younger generation didn't understand him and architecture suddenly changed completely,' says Lahti. 'Mies van der Rohe's influence was strong. It was quite hard for Aalto.' Laaksonen agrees. 'Aalto was used to being seen as modern and suddenly he was perceived as a dinosaur.' But he wasn't left out in the cold for long.

These days, Aalto's work is more revered than ever. The expression 'organic modernism' is sometimes used to describe his aesthetic, with its mix of stark functionality, tactile natural materials and soft organic forms.

That preference for natural materials, wood in particular, is a prevailing element of Finnish design and his philosophy on social architecture has never been more relevant. Studio Aalto in Helsinki has hundreds of global visitors every year. 'We will only start worrying if nobody comes any more,' says Laaksonen.

Below and right
Aalto built his studio in the Munkkiniemi district of Helsinki between 1954 and 1955 as his practice expanded and overflowed from the small studio in his home. Nautical shapes can be found throughout the design: the roof resembles a sail while the main room has a crow's nest-like balcony. Along with a studio, drawing room and reception room, it has a staff canteen called the Taverna, where Aalto would eat with his colleagues every day.

Above
The Paimio Chair is still in production today.

Top right
Completed relatively early in his career, the Paimio Sanatorium 1932 was arguably Alvar Aalto's most significant project.

Bottom right
Together with his wife Aino, Aalto designed all the sanitorium's furniture and interiors. The extent of the thoughtful detail he accomplished here came to define his all-encompassing approach to architecture. He designed floor lamps so that patients would not be disturbed by ceiling lights while lying on their beds, and wardrobes that were attached to the wall to allow easy cleaning beneath. Everything was considered.

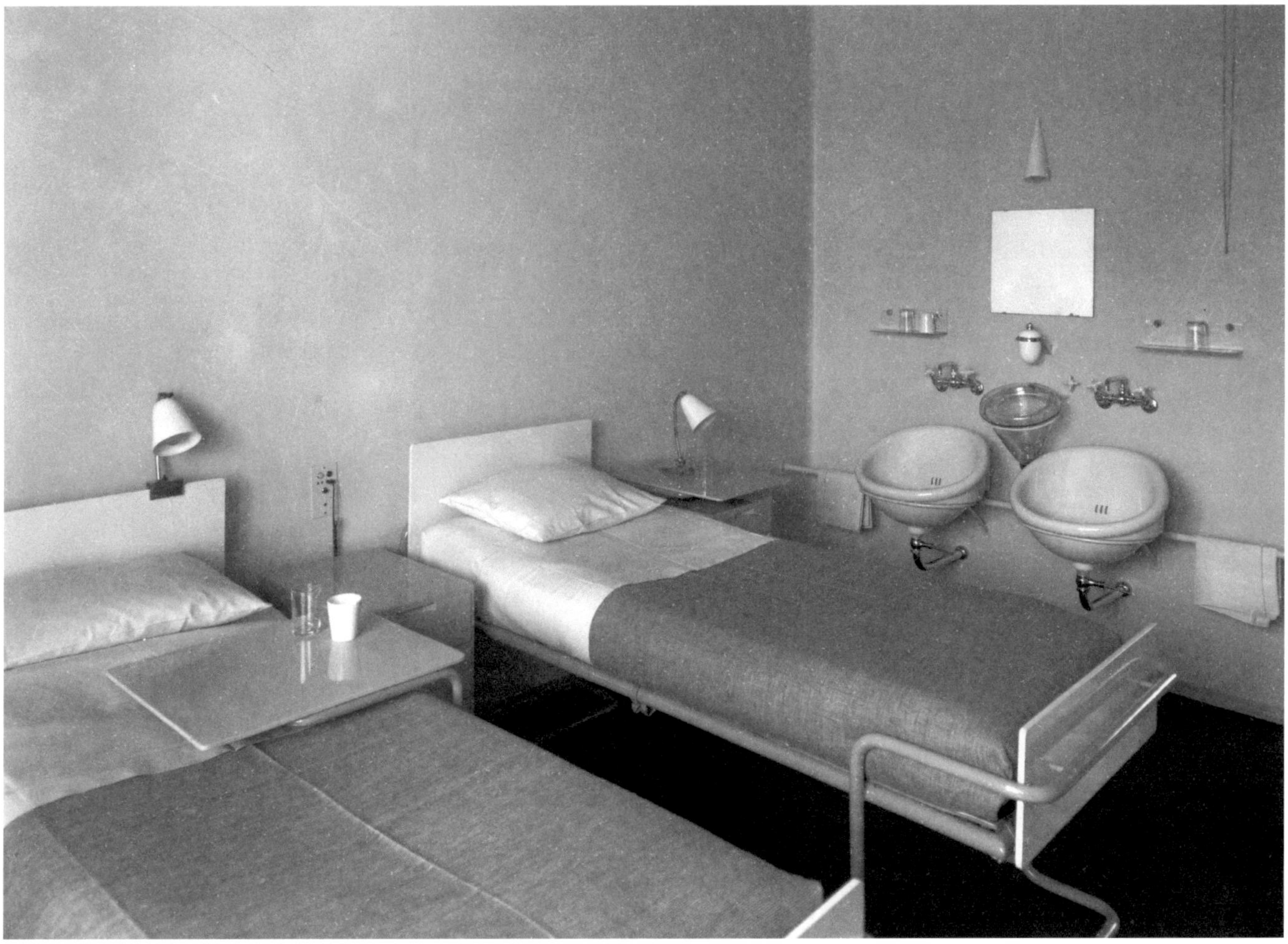

DEMOCRATIC DESIGN

DEMOCRATIC DESIGN

Above
Completed after Aalto's death in 1976, the Riola Parish Church 1978 in Italy reveals his mastery of perspective. Six concrete arches descend in size towards the altar, drawing the eye and the worshipper in.

Top right
The Viipuri Library 1935 in Russia boasts one of Aalto's best-known architectural features: the wave ceiling. It was installed for its excellent acoustic properties, although the wonderful sense of theatre created by the rolling form would not have escaped Aalto.

Bottom right
The undulating balconies of the Finlandia Hall 1967–71 project out over seating. By the time it was designed, Aalto had mastered the art of bending wood. The slat motif on the walls was intended to convey trees bending in the wind.

DEMOCRATIC DESIGN

Ilmari Tapiovaara's teacher told him to foster his creativity through private commissions and to avoid the restrictions of industry, but this was of no interest to this young and strong-willed creative who went on to be one of Finland's greatest industrial designers.

Tapiovaara subscribed to the modernist philosophy that good design should be available to the masses and he went on to design iconic, mass-produced furniture. Tapiovaara's innovations in manufacturing and design allowed him to make handsome but affordable furniture, and his techniques and principles are as valid today as ever.

THE CROWD PLEASER
ILMARI TAPIOVAARA

The ideals of modernism were at the forefront of Ilmari Tapiovaara's mind when he took a job in 1938 as artistic director at Asko, Finland's largest furniture manufacturer. In 1941, he became artistic and commercial director for the furniture company Keravan Puuteollisuus. In 1946, he and his wife Annikki Tapiovaara won a competition to design furniture for the Domus Academy, a new building to house the influx of students moving to Helsinki to study.

The famous Domus chair was one of the outcomes: a bentwood stacking chair with small flipper-like armrests, used as a work chair in student rooms, hallways, auditoriums and canteens. The chair was put into serial production, and became Finland's first international post-war hit.

During the 1950s, Tapiovaara became prolific. In 1951 he and his wife established their own office, and together they designed extensively for public premises, such as schools, universities, banks, offices, hotels and even for the Finnish army. Tapiovaara pioneered furniture that reflected modern life: flat-packed to make distribution more efficient and built using streamlined production processes to reduce the price. The super-light Fanett chair, for example, is pressed in one piece, making it cheap to mass-produce and affordable to buy.

Tapiovaara recognised the limits of the Finnish market and the importance of treating the world as his market instead. He worked abroad in various roles, including as a professor at the School of Design of the Illinois Institute of Technology in Chicago from 1952 to 1953, and then in Paraguay and Mauritius, designing furniture on behalf of a U.N. development programme.

Above
A master craftsman, Tapiovaara also understood consumerism, as this advert for the Mademoiselle lounge chair 1956 shows.

Left
The success of Tapiovaara's design work is its timeless, universal quality. Human in scale and function, there is a charm and accessibility about designs, such as the Ovalette table 1954, the Pirkka chairs and bar stool 1955 that endeared them to consumers.

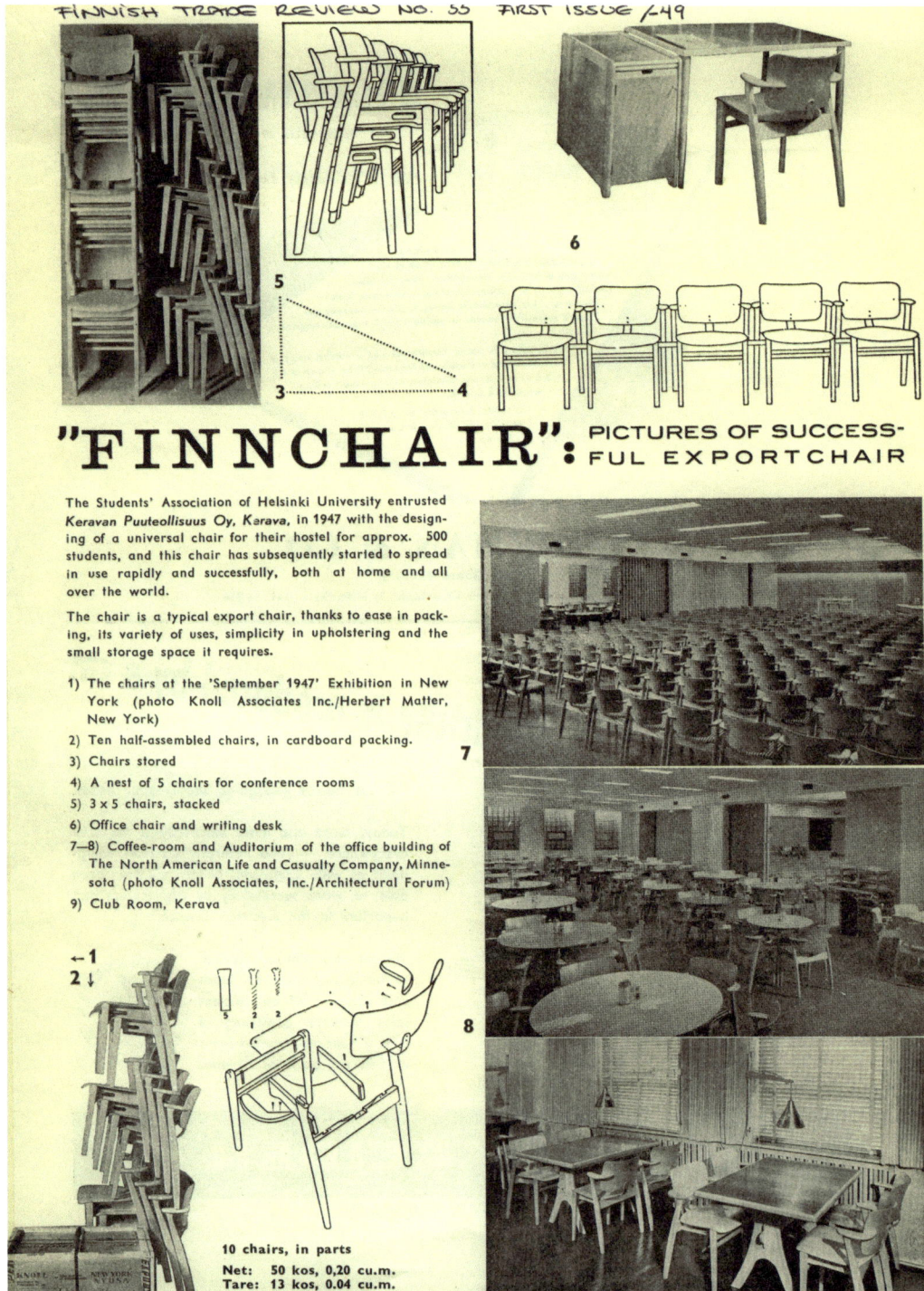

Above
Universities, schools and public buildings were Tapiovaara's main market. The Finnchair is one example of his workhorse designs. He even designed the Root Table 1941, made from cheap fir wood using traditional techniques, for the Finnish Army barracks.

Right
Tubular steel and bent wood, as used here in the NANA chair 1957 and the Tee Tee occasional table 1940, were Tapiovaara's most often used materials.

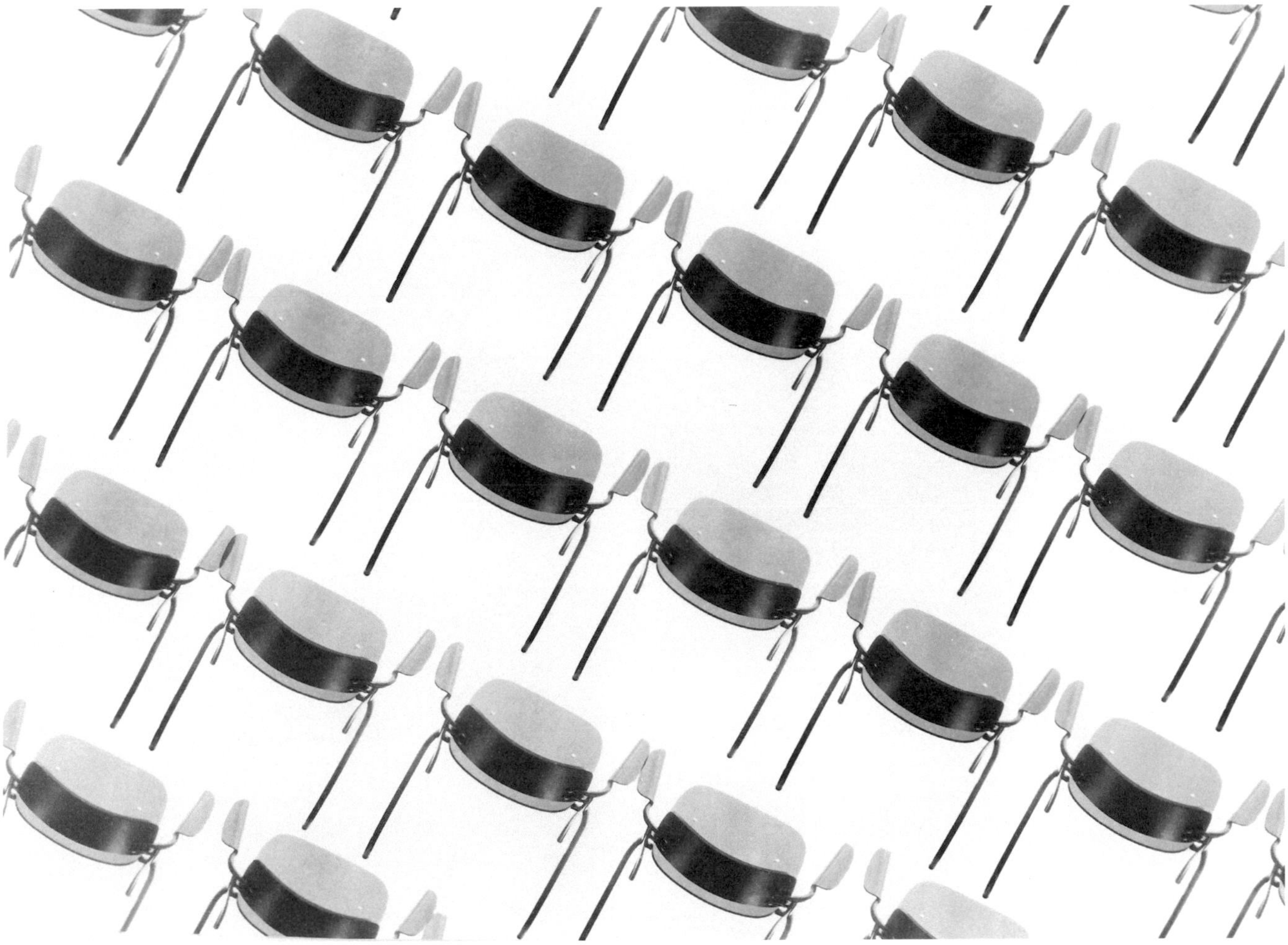

DEMOCRATIC DESIGN

Arabia, Fiskars, Nokia… All are recognised internationally as manufacturers and design companies, but in Finland they're known as points on a map too. Ceramic maker Arabia has been at the forefront of Finnish industrial design since the last century. It gained special significance when Kaj Franck came on board in the 1950s with a set of values and ambitions that would reverberate throughout Finnish industry. Today, Arabia is part of a bigger family of brands that fall under the ownership of Fiskars.

Fiskars is Finland's oldest company and a producer of tools, most famously scissors, named after the small village where it originated as an ironworks in 1649. Also in the family is Iittala, another more-than-familiar tableware brand. Together, Arabia and Iittala dominate this market, both abroad and at home, and both produce their ceramics, glassware and accessories side by side at Arabia's famous factory in the area of Arabia, just outside Helsinki.

BEAUTIFYING THE EVERYDAY
ARABIA AND IITTALA

The Arabia factory's iconic chimneys still tower over the surrounding area. It has been a hive of industrial activity since it was built in 1874 as an outpost of Rörstrand, a Swedish company that set up shop here to secure Russian trade. Rörstrand's range of wares included art pottery, domestic and utilityware, sanitaryware, tiles and bricks.

During the First World War, Arabia passed into Finnish hands. In 1929, the factory introduced its first tunnel kiln, helping it to become one of the world's largest pottery manufacturers. But it was only when Swedish moderniser Kurt Ekholm became its artistic director in 1932 that the brand began to resemble the one we know today. He introduced studios to the factory, uniting art and industry, and, crucially, appointed a chief designer. By chance, Ekholm had been out rowing with Kaj Franck and he joked that the young designer would be a natural on a potters' wheel, as he kept turning the boat in circles. It turned out that he was right and Franck joined Arabia in 1945.

Franck's strong social conscience was fuelled by the Second World War. He was interested in mass-production and technology's potential to produce diverse, streamlined, practical objects at a reasonable price: democratic design. Others shared his goal and aided by a surge of post-war prosperity, designers and manufacturers in Finland set about putting this philosophy into practice and creating objects for the home. Franck's modular tableware series Kilta, later relaunched as Teema, is an icon of this period. The first of its kind, it allowed customers to choose their own combination depending on their wants and needs. Over the next 20 years it sold 25 million pieces.

Arabia ceramics have taken many forms. Iittala, its partner tableware and glassworks brand, is held in equally high esteem: another flagship for the values of Finnish design. The two brands have worked with some of Finland's most talented designers—Aino and Alvar Aalto, Oiva Toikka, Tapio Wirkkala and others—and they nurture and provide a platform for today's young designers too. They have shown a strong awareness of their role within everyday Finnish life, from Iittala's 'beautifying the everyday' project of the 1950s to today's philosophy of mix-and-match designs.

Previous page
The chimney of the Arabia factory is a much-loved landmark. The company is named after the Arabia area which, legend has it, was named by a returning sailor who had recently travelled to the Middle East. Others say its exotic name was the result of its distance from the city centre.

Right and following page
The Arabia factory produces a varied mix of ceramic designs. Each begins with a plaster mould, which makes around 100 pieces before being replaced.

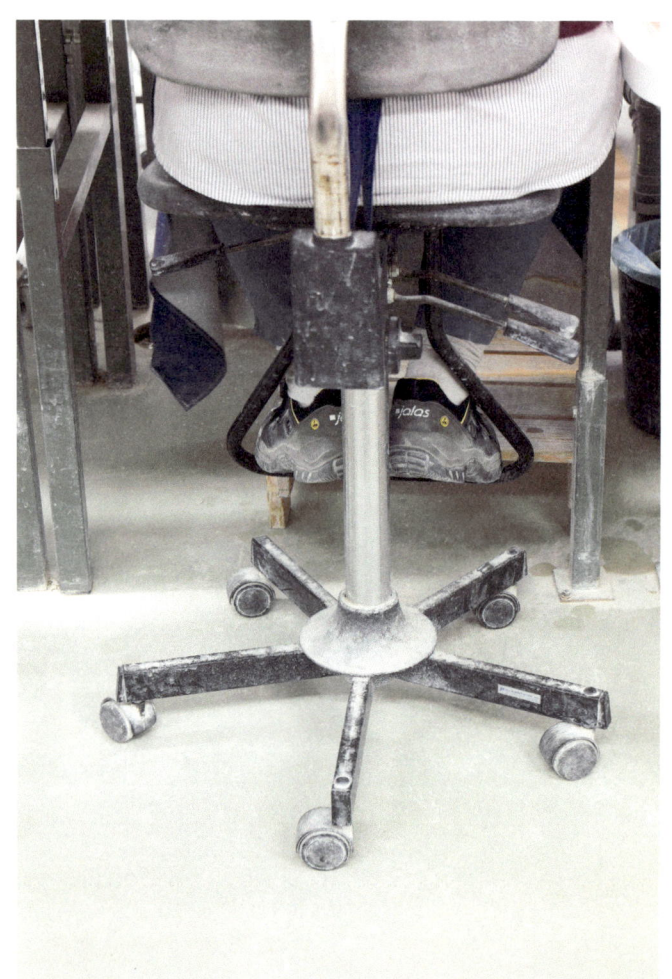

ARABIA AND IITTALA

Above
The Paratiisi design was created by Birger Kaipiainen in 1970. Kaipiainen was a master of applied decoration, but the industrial designs that have become household favourites in Finland barely hint at his extraordinary studio work: his giant ceramic murals and surreal, fantastical designs were far ahead of his time.

Left
These designs from the 1970s show just one type of applied decoration from Arabia's very extensive back catalogue. It ranges from ornate Russian-style patterns to rustic designs to floral motifs, not forgetting The Moomins, who first graced Arabia crockery in the 1950s.

ARABIA AND IITTALA

1929–1941

1953

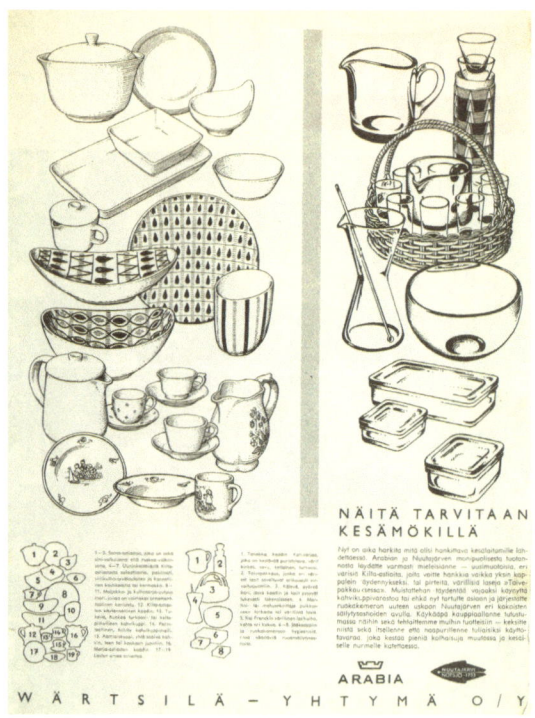

1955

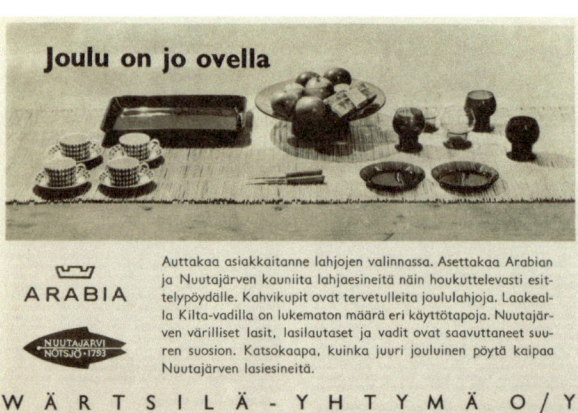

1956

Arabia's archive is rich with material from its history. Its posters and sales catalogues demonstrate how the company developed products to meet evolving demand.

1957

1958

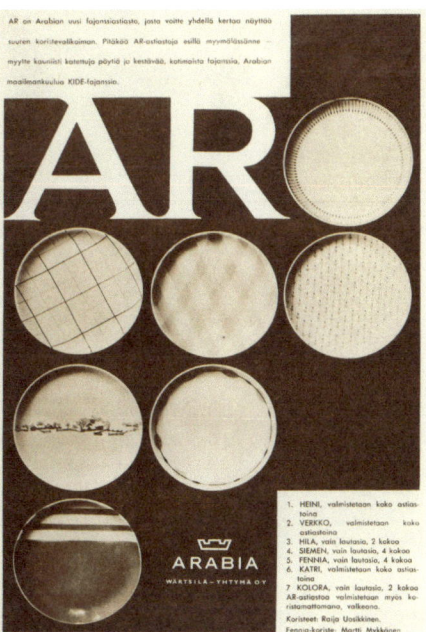

1959

1961

Iittala uses various methods to produce its glassware. Although it pioneered industrialisation with pressed glass, some of its designs are still handblown, such as the iconic Savoy Vase 1936 by Alvar Aalto. It takes seven craftsmen to make each one.

Above
Alvar Aalto's original name for his Savoy Vase design was Eskimo Woman's Leather Breeches. Whatever the inspiration, it has become one of the best known of all Finnish designs. Its organic, flowing form is a reference point for the connection between Finnish landscape and design objects. A social observer once said that in order to be truly Finnish, one had to own a Savoy Vase.

Right
Iittala's Sarjaton collection clearly articulates the company's contemporary concerns. It was designed by a collective of designers, including non-industrial designers, such as Aleksi Kuokka, Musuta and Samuji, who worked with Harri Koskinen. It includes glass, ceramic and wooden pieces: the ultimate in flexible, adaptable tableware.

Finland is often spoken of as a 'land of extremes.' On the one hand there is the stereotype of reserved, quiet people shaped by dark, cold winters. On the other, there is a wealth of individual thinking, and daring design and innovation. Just as those winters find their antithesis in glorious, light-filled summers, Finnish reserve is juxtaposed with boldness and progress. A folkloric attitude to heroisicm and storytelling permeates contemporary designs.

A key Finnish word used to describe the national character is sisu, which essentially means determination, strength of will and perseverance. That against-the-odds, hardy and gritty attitude helps explain much about the Finns, from their love of extreme sports and experiences, such as ice swimming, to the dedication behind wonderfully inventive creations. Today's young Finnish designers are especially determined to make their mark.

THE EPIC AND THE BOLD

Sanna Annukka's prints are quintessentially contemporary Finnish. She uses bold colour and a stylised graphic language in her fabric designs and illustrative works. Her most recent creations for Finnish design powerhouse Marimekko are a case in point. Annuka's trademark motifs are representations of the animals and landscape of her homeland: birds recur particularly often. Annuka dreams of owning a little house in Lapland but currently lives in the U.K.

DRAWN FROM NATURE
SANNA ANNUKKA

When did you first get involved with illustration? What drew you to it?

I wanted to be an artist from a very young age. Being creative was what made me happiest. It wasn't until my foundation course that I decided to go down the illustration route. Up until that point I was tempted by photography, and textiles too. I loved it all.

Illustration won me over in the end as the best solution, as I felt I could continue experimenting with different media. I went on to study on the Illustration BA (Hons) course at the University of Brighton. It was there that I discovered my love of printmaking.

What do you find particularly interesting about your chosen medium? And when are you satisfied with what you've created?

I love seeing my work screen-printed. It develops a new personality and has more character than when seen digitally. The process is therapeutic—watching layer after of vibrant colour build up and form an image—albeit a little back-breaking at times.

I am never fully satisfied with what I've created. There comes a point when I have to accept my designs for what they are, rather than to strive for perfection every time.

How long did it take you to perfect your craft? Or are you always learning?

I haven't perfected anything yet. I'm definitely still learning. The learning side of it never stops, and it shouldn't. Artists should never get complacent with their work.

Is there a particular process, in terms of thought and craft, that you go through when you're tackling a project?

I love making mood boards, particularly if I'm designing products or fabric patterns. I often have so many ideas and thoughts whirling around in my head that I need to display them in a more organised fashion. That's where mood boards come in.

Do you feel more comfortable working in 2D or 3D?

Most of my work is 2D, but in recent years I have got more into product design, which I love. However, I'm still only involved with the 2D process of my product design. For instance, I don't physically cut out my Soul Birds from wood myself. That would be disastrous.

I am interested in working properly in 3D and so I'm on the brink of joining a ceramics course. It's a constant fascination to see how I can translate my style into different media. Some of my idols were ceramic artists, so I have a particular fondness for the medium.

What piece of work are you most proud of?

I still hold dear my Kanteleen Kutsu fabric pattern for Marimekko. Being such a fan of folklore, in particular Finland's national epic The Kalevala, it was a wonderful opportunity to translate some of my most treasured parts of the epic into modern fabric patterns. It hadn't been done before. Kanteleen Kutsu depicts the heroic character of Väinämöinen who plays a harp made from pike bones. The music is so beautiful that it entices forest creatures from far and wide to gather and marvel at the songs.

I haven't perfected anything yet. I'm definitely still learning. The learning side of it never stops, and it shouldn't.

SANNA ANNUKKA

Previous page
Kanteleen Kutsu pattern 2009 for Marimekko depicting a scene from The Kalevala

Above
Sanna Annukka

Right
Vanhakaupunki pattern 2012 for Marimekko

What helps your creativity?
Reading, writing, travelling—particularly holidays in Lapland. But also complete time out from being creative helps too. Give me a couple of weeks off from doing anything remotely creative, and by the end of it I'm charged up, eager and raring to go again.

How do you turn inspiration into craft?
Writers write. Artists draw!

The challenge of creating something new is intense. How do you come up with something different and special?
It's the biggest challenge for an artist to keep coming up with new ideas. Luckily I don't feel like I'm running out of ideas yet. The key is knowing where to look for inspiration and that should always come from your passions.

How do you think your nationality affects your work?
My Finnish heritage has a huge influence on my work. It's a beautiful country: it's the land of a thousand lakes, of age-old granite rock and never-ending forest. Fishing trips to Lapland during my childhood years have left such an impression on me: the midnight sun, the wildlife, the landscapes… There is so much to draw inspiration from.

How often do you go back to Finland? And does this stimulate your work?
I try to go at least a few times a year and to Lapland every other year. My last trip to Lapland inspired my second collection for Marimekko, in particular my pattern Kultakero, which depicts rolling fells and ancient forests. A classic Lappish landscape.

If you lived there, do you think your work would seem less Finnish?
I get asked this a lot. I just don't know. Sure, living in England means I can be in a bit of a romantic bubble with my representations of Finland. I'd like to buy a cottage in Lapland one day. But I can only imagine that that will inspire my work further.

What do you think Finnish design represents? And what does it mean to you?
Some of the most famous artworks, whether it be glasswork, architecture, furniture, ceramics or textiles, carry a strong essence of Finnish landscape within them. An example is Tapio Wirkkala's beautiful glasswork which was often influenced by melting ice forms. I think the majority of Finnish design draws inspiration from the natural environment and so Finnish design to me represents the bond between nature and man.

Why do you think Finns are known for their design?
Because of an ability to create such a strong Finnish essence. I like to think everyone is nourished by nature, and so design inspired by nature simply connects with people. It is appealing.

What would you like people to know about Finnish design?
It's often a celebration, often a reflection, but always a sincere response to the native land and its environment.

This page
Kultakero pattern for Marimekko.

Right
Soul Birds are a frequent motif in Annukka's work.

Soul Birds are based on the myth of the sielulintu, which is believed to deliver the soul to a person when they are born, to protect it when they are asleep and to transport it to the afterlife when they die.

Living in England means I can be in a bit of a romantic bubble with my representations of Finland.

SANNA ANNUKKA

Today's generation of product designers have a whole host of challenges to face, and a rich design heritage to live up to. The lack of local manufacturers is a problem for those who want to keep their design skills close to home and the potent legacy of Finland's historic master designers is, at least in some minds, as much a hurdle to be overcome as a help.

While the characteristics and values of Finland's design past may not always be immediately apparent in the motivations of young designers, there are constants. The large number of design collectives is a manifestation of the community spirit that has always infused Finnish crafts. And traditional methods of making and materials continue to inspire, as do Finland's unique culture and environment.

THE RISING TIDE
YOUNG FINNISH DESIGNERS

Clockwise, from top left
Matti Syrjälä, Kaamos.

Saara Renvall, Imu Design.

Mika Tolvanen, Rehti.

Mari Isopahkala.

KAAMOS

Kaamos is a collective made up of five young, independent designers: Erik Bertell, Vesa Kattelus, Katriina Nuutinen, Anna Palomaa and Matti Syrjälä. They have all come together to exhibit and promote their work, citing a healthy admiration for Finnish culture and traditional methods of making as a unifying factor.

How does being a collective affect what you do?
Erik Bertell: Well, I suppose we have chosen this particular viewpoint: that defines a lot of our work. I think one of the factors that is defining for our collective is about coming up with concepts, instead of just making some stuff and trying to bind it together afterwards. Last autumn in Paris, for example, we had an exhibition where we built an installation on the theme of traditional Finnish summer cottage culture.

Is there a practical motivation to working together?
Vesa Kattelus: It helps immensely with everything. There are all the practical issues and because each of us has different strengths it makes it easier to apply for grants. It can be useful having all these different skills. Erik is a graphic designer, for example.

Tell me about the influence of traditions on your work.
Anna Palomaa: I heard a story from the Sami people about the days when they were wandering after their reindeers. They had a box for porcelain coffee cups so that when their guests came from the south they could offer coffee as a sign of their hospitality.

What is your opinion on recent Finnish design history? Do you take inspiration from it, or are you looking further afield for your influences?
EB: It's a good thing that we have this strong foundation of design and industry here—but it's not always good. When you flip through a magazine you constantly see the same objects. So even though we have so many people working in the field of design, the spotlight is really narrow. That's a little bit frustrating. When companies want to produce something new they'd rather find something from the 1950s than go to a young designer and ask, can you do something for us?

How is your work received abroad? Is the fact that you come from Finland an advantage?
AP: I don't know. We like to try to stay a bit further away from the most obvious perceptions if we can. I think we try to position ourselves somewhere further from the epicentre of this Scandinavian modernist scene.

Above
**Hely jewel light 2009
by Katriina Nuutinen.**

Right, clockwise from top left
**Tatti containers 2013
by Katriina Nuutinen.**

**Riuku chair 2011
by Matti Syrjälä.**

**Säilö container set 2013
by Matti Syrjälä.**

THE EPIC AND THE BOLD

SAARA RENVALL AND IMU

Imu Design is one of Helsinki's most established design groups. Several years ago, designers Saara Renvall, Elina Aalto and Krista Kosonen decided to create a platform for Finland's young designers. As well as producing work themselves, they promote the work of others and help forge relationships between the new generation and Finnish manufacturers. Independently, Renvall works with many traditional producers and has a fondness for textile design.

What is Imu?

Imu is not an organisation; it's not a company. It's just three of us. It was started in 2002. We were all studying. I think everybody was grappling with the same problem: what should we do?

There weren't really jobs for us. You realise, when you look back at the time when we started Imu, there weren't groups like us or anybody promoting. Now it's really common. There are a lot of people doing things together, going abroad and making exhibitions, which is good. Imu encouraged people to do their own thing, and not just follow what is taught to be good design.

Did you plan to manufacture products too?

Obviously that was our aim. But we didn't make any plans. I think our internet page looks so professional that at one point people thought we were a company. But I think it's OK like this. I don't want to run a design company, manufacturing things.

Tell me about the Protoshop event. When did it begin, and how did it come about?

With the Protoshop we meet every now and then and we organise. We just had a jury for new works and we selected 10 pieces. We organise it every year. The idea of Protoshop is that a company can come and buy a product by one of the young designers for their own collection. And the designers get some publicity as well.

And you still think it's important to give a helping hand to those younger designers? Is it any easier for them now than when you first started?

I think it's maybe easier. But I still don't think it's easy. But the younger generation, they are more motivated, they know what they want and they are eager to get it. In that sense, I think they're doing a better job.

In terms of manufacturing, do you mean bigger factories? Or small workshops?

Yes, both. But I guess now what I see are people turning back and saying: 'Hey, we have to do something to keep the industry.' I think that's something that is really interesting, in all countries. Because then you get the local flavour as well. I hope that is the case, because I think in Finland we follow a little bit what's happening in other places. It's hard to get that balance.

Tell me a little about your textile projects.

I've always been interested in textiles. Unfortunately, I've seen in Finland, and even my professor has said to me, that women who study textiles are not that appreciated. Hard materials, furniture or wood or metal are ranked so much higher. I think that's a shame. There's something about textiles that is so right for today. I think that's super-interesting. A hundred years ago, all the women in Finland knew how to weave because everything was made at home. I guess now it's a good time to look back, because there's a need for a certain kind of softness and easiness and homely things.

Tell me about your recent projects.

I have done some work with Friends of Finnish Handicrafts, which is one of the oldest companies in Finland. It's been around for 130 years. It's been a really interesting adventure to go into that world. I will be trying to make sure that the company will run for the next 130 years.

Are craft brands popular? Does the younger generation appreciate them?

I think more now, yes. I don't think you can be a designer in this time and not have knowledge about these things. Otherwise you're off the train already. Design education used to be based on this training in craftsmanship. And design came from doing that. I think we have lost that a little bit, because it's so easy to go to the computer and everything looks so finished already thanks to beautiful rendering programmes.

Clockwise, from top left
Hide storage basket.

Aava home collection, designed with Elina Helenius.

Nappi sofa 2010 for Suomi Soffa, designed with Elina Helenius.

MIKA TOLVANEN

Mika Tolvanen is enjoying a steady rise to acclaim as an internationally significant designer. His Visu chairs and other projects for Scandinavian brand Muuto are designs that most would consider to be quintessentially Nordic in their comfortable, easy functionality.

Are you working with Muuto at the moment?
Yes. This Visu chair is my third product for them. I just started doing the fourth, a table.

And a lamp?
The Koho lamp is for Italian brand FontanaArte. They're trying to reinvigorate an old brand.

Are there any local manufacturers you are working with?
I'm working with my first Finnish customer now. It is a small company, Keraplast, that makes lamps.

Your manufacturers are an international lot then?
Yes. There is a lot of emailing! But if you have a good collaborator to talk with about the technical stuff, then that improves the end product a lot.

You have said of your design philosophy that 'what really defines objects is how we use them, not what they appear to be. Design should not be the one that requires attention by being special.' How does that translate into your work?
If you have a stool, but you use it as a low table, then by nature it is a low table. I do not wish to make extravagant objects. I find these objects unnatural, and often very unusable. How this translates to my work is perhaps most evident in the simple forms of my designs. They often have nothing extra on them, just what you need. But making objects simple is the hardest thing to achieve.

What is happening in Finnish design at the moment, in your opinion? There are a lot of young designers—and suddenly a lot of Finnish groups too. For example, you are part of a collective, Rehti. Why are there so many?
It's so far away here, so we have to have groups. And most Finnish designers are friends, particularly in Helsinki.

Do you still find it a good place to be?
Yes. I have a good support system here. And there are grants we can apply for.

Do you see your work as being part of any kind of bigger Nordic tradition?
I hadn't thought about that. I guess if it happens, it's happening naturally.

Above
Koho lamp 2013 for FontanaArte.

Top right
Visu chair 2012 for Muuto.

Bottom right
Vuoka lamp prototype 2005.

> **I do not wish to make extravagant objects. I find these objects unnatural and often very unusable.**
>
> MIKA TOLVANEN

MARI ISOPAHKALA

Mari Isopahkala works with all manner of materials and scales. While her work demonstrates some characteristic Finnish design traits, such as being inspired by nature, in many other aspects it does not. Instead, she chooses to follow her instincts and work with projects and people that give her new challenges.

You design a whole range of objects. Do you have a particularly curious mind?
I graduated from the University of Art and Design in 2008, so I've been working for around five years. I do various things, including product design and some spatial design. The scale is more or less the scale of a human, so that can be everything from jewellery to the kitchen. It is interesting to work with different materials.

What is it like to produce things here in Finland? Can you find workshops and manufacturers to work with?
It's not so easy. I've been working to find my crew: people who know me and know how to do things. It takes a lot of time. You have to be a detective. It is really a huge part of working as a designer, to find the workers.

What materials are you currently exploring?
Crystal, and I work with jewellery too. It's a really new thing for me because I'm a natural designer but I haven't graduated as a goldsmith. You need to think a lot about function. I didn't really realise that before. Jewellery designs are modular; made up of a composite of parts. The jewellery-maker Lapona's works are always inspired by Finnish nature and things like that. My newest piece is called Soma and is inspired by the boats that transport logs on the river.

You rolled your eyes when you said Finnish nature! Is that just because it's such a common cliché for designers?
Yes it is, but I still do it! All the time!

What would you like to be designing or doing next?
I don't know. I feel I'm quite modest in the sense that I'm just happy if I can continue like this.

Is the relationship with industry important in what you do?
Yes, in a sense. With the jewellery, for example, I could make some studio pieces myself but somehow it's really nice to work with a team. If I don't trust or like the people who I work with, you can see it in the product. My design for Marimekko, a set of stainless steel cutlery, has just launched. That was a nice process. You can see that people love what they do there and it was really fun.

Was it good to work with such a big Finnish design name?
Yes. And for me the Marimekko cutlery was interesting because they didn't have anything like it before so they were fresh. That's nice.

Does the accessibility of your designs concern you?
I don't think about it, because it's very natural for me to make something really functional. But what I bring to design is maybe not so much about mass production; it doesn't have to be so everyday in that sense. It can also be really personal. There are some characters and stories that I want to express in my works and I don't mind if it is not 'Nordic design'. But maybe it has something extra.

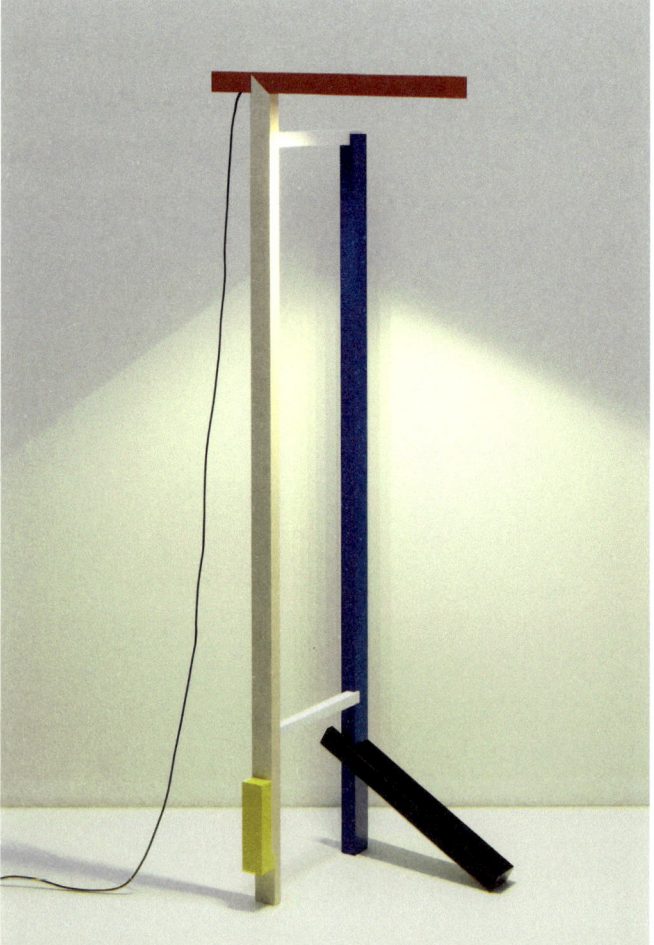

Above
Ojentaa 2 sculptural floor light 2013.

Right
Fatty 1 art glass 2012.

AALTO UNIVERSITY

Most of Finland's home-grown design talents will have passed through the halls of the former University of Art and Design, now the Aalto University, in Helsinki. Established in 2010, Aalto University is the product of three highly regarded, historic universities joining forces: Helsinki School of Economics, Helsinki University of Technology and the University of Art and Design Helsinki.

Like its partners, the University of Art and Design Helsinki was a leader in its field. Founded as the Craft School in 1871, it counts Tapio Wirkkala, Timo Sarpaneva and Kaj Franck among its alumni. Many of its talented students would later return to teach new generations of aspiring craftsmen and designers: the energetic and creative spirit of the school and its tutors was a driving force in creating the exciting, innovative design of the last century. Far from resting on its heritage, today it is the largest school of art and design in the Nordic countries, with almost 3,000 students studying its broad range of courses.

The school has a strong focus on cross-collaboration, as its multi-disciplinary show at the Milan Furniture Fair in 2013 demonstrated. Called Norther, a reference to a sudden and stabbing northern wind, the show presented an edit of 26 fresh ideas from students working in furniture design, ceramics and glass art, industrial design, textile art, fashion and clothing design. 'The exhibits reflect our teaching philosophy, which combines a strong, original artistic vision with insightful technical implementation,' explains Professor Jouko Järvisalo.

Top right
Three Cups 2013
by Anna Van der Lei
and Laura Timosaari.

Bottom right
Bumpy 2013
by Kristos Mavrostomos.

Below
Pala textile 2013
by Hanna Anonen.

ALVAR AALTO UNIVERSITY

Our teaching philosophy combines a strong, original artistic vision with insightful technical implementation.

PROFESSOR JOUKO JÄRVISALO

Top left
Keno 2013
by Noora Liesimaa.

Bottom left
Avaa 2013
by Nina Kosonen.

Above
Various tableware including Maja Series 2013 by Pekka Kuivamaki, 3 Cups 2013 by Anna Van der Lei and Laura Timosaari and Bumpy Glasses 2013 by Kristos Mavrostomos.

WOODISM

At first glance, the Woodism design collective might look like they are doing nothing new: wooden furniture is, after all, a staple of Finnish design. But it's the way in which designers Tapio Anttila, Merita Soini and carpenter Markku Tonttila source their raw material that is the innovation here. Woodism makes use of felled urban trees from parks and pavements in Helsinki, saving the material from the chipper and offering it an unexpected respect.

The project began in 2007. 'At that time people were upset that some old trees in Helsinki's Kaivopuisto Park had been axed down,' says Tapio Anttila. 'We wanted to give the trees a new life.' He describes how the old trees offer a character that farmed wood does not possess. 'We look at the tree and let it define the design. What is usually considered a fault is a decoration for us.'

The material is unpredictable, gnarled and often comes in curious forms. But this is the appeal for the collective who describe their urban wood as having 'personality'. Many of their clients are ordinary people who need to get rid of a tree in their back yard but do not want to dump it. Instead they ask Woodism to make furniture from it for them.

Anttila believes that Woodism represents a journey back to basics. 'But this is not Finnish design in a traditional sense,' he says. 'It's actually quite the opposite.'

Below
Palikka–Rahit (block footstools) by Merita Soini and Tapio Anttila.

Right
Tuolit & Pöytä (Chairs and Table) by Susan Elo.

THE EPIC AND THE BOLD

We look at the tree and let it define the design. What is usually considered a fault is a decoration for us.

TAPIO ANTTILA

Womenswear designer Samu-Jussi Koski produces beautiful, classic clothes to suit all women. He repeats his staple designs continually, adding flourishes with seasonal collections. The Samuji take on everyday classics is not dissimilar to the industrial design values so prevalent in Finland.

That fact might be explained by his long stint as first designer and then creative director at Marimekko. His refreshingly democratic and ethical approach to making fashion has earned him a host of loyal, local followers from every generation who appreciate his concept of design and love his clothes.

DRESSING EVERYWOMAN
SAMUJI

What inspired your fashion label?
I had been at Marimekko for almost 10 years and I had been thinking that I wanted to do my own thing, my own concept. At the same time I was a little bit disappointed about the fashion world: how it works, the manufacturing and production and everything. It was midsummer when I left. I was in a midsummer sauna, which is a very iconic thing in Finland, and I was thinking about my life. I realised that maybe I needed to change some things. Why only complain if I don't do anything about the situation?

So you founded Samuji. Your idea was always about making things differently right from the start.
Ethics-wise, yes. I wanted to do things really well. I wanted to make things in places where I knew people and I also wanted to give production back to Europe. I wanted to have production in Finland, but that is really difficult nowadays. And I think that customers are not the ones that should be aware. We should be, we who are producing stuff. So that was the starting point.

And then I started to think that we really don't need anything new, so I wanted to make things that were more permanent, and so I created a staple wardrobe. I interviewed my friends who are different kinds of women from different age groups and different economic or social groups and asked them, if you could choose only 10 pieces for the rest of your life, what would they be? Actually, it was quite easy for everyone and they were saying almost the same thing. And then because I wanted to do something more creative as well I made the other section which was seasonal and more colourful.

And has the concept been well received? Do people like this approach?
Yes. I'm happy. It was the right thing to do because, like everything in this world, it's really intuitive.

And your seasonal collections? Where do you get your inspiration for those?
From everywhere: when I'm travelling, but also from Finland and from nature, of course. Every Finnish person says that. Music, films, people, friends… And fabrics, textiles too: that is definitely one of the strongest aspects of the brand, and that's what the customers notice.

Who are your customers?
Usually a woman who is very well aware of herself and her surroundings. She could be anywhere between 20 and 60, 70 even. It's so nice to see.

You said before that you were producing some things in Finland. What are those?
Some woollens and some cotton shirts that were made by a family company that is 130 years old—although, sadly, it just closed. But there are still some small producers. We just found a beading factory and our leather is from Finland as well. It is reindeer leather: really ecological.

Above
Samu-Jussi Koski.

Right
Samuji's evocative imagery captures the carefree spirit of the brand. There is no pretension or loftiness in this fashion house.

These things are functional and at the same time they are really beautiful. And that is the core of what we try to do.

SAMU-JUSSI KOSKI

> **I'm not that creative, actually. What I mean is, I make basic clothes with nice fabrics. I consider the commercial aspect: is this something that people want to buy?**
>
> SAMU-JUSSI KOSKI

It isn't only women's fashion that you're interested in. What else do you think Samuji might produce?
We are starting a men's line. It is a natural way to expand. And we've been thinking a lot about an interiors line.

You're no stranger to product design either, having recently worked on the Sarjaton collection for Iittala.
Yes. We created the whole concept together, but in the end it was only one print from us that was used. I got the idea for the project because I am always collecting things from flea markets and antique shops, or buying something new and mixing them together. So we were thinking that was a new idea for a collection of objects.

How does your creative process work?
I'm not that creative, actually. What I mean is, I make basic clothes with nice fabrics. I consider the commercial aspect: is this something that people want to buy?

That approach is familiar when talking about Finnish design: producing good design for everyday use.
Yes. If you think about the Iittala glasses we are using here, for example, these things are functional and at the same time they are really beautiful. And that is the core of what we try to do as well.

You often use iconic Finnish architecture as your backdrop. What is the idea behind the Samuji imagery?
We still have some dreams of places to shoot in, but we haven't got the permission. We've shot in Jan Anderson's house in Turku, at Eliel Saarinen's home and also at Alvar Aalto's home. I'm a really big fan of Alvar Aalto and so it was a big honour to shoot there.

What makes you such a fan of his?
I think for the same things, the philosophy, that we've just talked about. The idea of making something for everyday: simple, functional objects. And for thinking about details; all the details are incredible. In clothing it is the same: it has to be functional. I think that's really important. Also the fabric, the quality: it should have a timelessness.

Previous page and right
Choosing to use iconic Finnish locations such as the home of Alvar Aalto, seen here as the backdrop for the Fall 2013 collection, firmly places the brand within the cultural and creative landscape of Finland.

THE EPIC AND THE BOLD

The Ivana Helsinki fashion label began as a personal art project. Paola Suhonen merged the disciplines that interested her—painting, textile design, fashion and, later, film—to create expressive collections of clothes that were rich in narrative. Recently Suhonen has scooped up awards for her film, fashion and a prestigious Pro Finlandia medal.

Today, each Ivana Helsinki collection is presented as a complete story, often with accompanying film, installation and photography. Suhonen weaves many different cultural influences into her crafted stories, with her home town of Helsinki a recurring motif, proudly expressed in the label's name.

TELLING TALES
IVANA HELSINKI

What are the cornerstones of the brand?
There are four legs that the brand stands on: film, fashion, design and art. It is still my personal art project. And I never follow the fashion trends; the latest silhouettes. It is more about stories.

Tell me about your interest in storytelling.
I never actually think, OK, I want to tell stories. It just comes quite naturally. When I start a collection I like digging into my own memories for inspiration. The work has an intimate personal layer.

Can you give me an example?
A recent print for a collection was called Mourning Sun Motel. I had heard there had been a solar eclipse in the late 1800s, which happened on the same day as our midsummer festival: the biggest festival of eternal light, of sunshine, in Finland. I'm not even sure if the story is true, but that was the trigger. And I'm a huge motel fan: I've travelled across the States, I think, seven times.

I turned the story into a film. Those elements were woven into the script and then we shot this melancholic film in 3D. And I like that connection: you watch the sun eclipse with dark glasses and you watch 3D movies with glasses too.

Why did you chose to name the brand after the city?
Back then, no fashion designer in Finland would say that they were from here. They were ashamed to be from Helsinki. For me, I really feel that there is a super-cool cross-cultural thing in Finland: the eastern flavour coming from the Russian side and then this Scandinavian mood too.

Do you take any inspiration from other Finnish creatives or artists?
Yes. I love the 1950s glassware designers: people like Oiva Toikka and Kaj Franck. There is something dark in their design that I find really fascinating. I love the mixture of having something decorative and something super-pure and simple and functional. It is a talent to do something that is between these two directions and that has an edge.

What do you think about the Finnish fashion scene? Has it changed since Ivana Helsinki was launched?
I don't feel that I'm a part of the fashion scene in that way. But there is a younger generation: there are a lot of designers who are really talented and working for other larger companies abroad.

Do you think the heritage of design is helpful to the younger generation and their creative ambitions?
Yes. I think that is a great base. Although Finland's reputation for high-quality design lies back in the 1950s, so we can't just rely on that. We need to develop and work hard to do new things. That is our challenge.

Above
Paola Suhonen.

Right
The Mourning Sun Hotel 2013 collection merges references gathered from Suhonen's recent road trips in the U.S. and floral motifs that are purely Finnish.

I love the mixture of having something decorative and something super-pure and simple and functional.

IVANA HELSINKI

Romanticism and storytelling are at the heart of the collections. The Indian Summer 2012 collection imagery is typically dream-like and ethereal.

PHOTOGRAPHY CREDITS

Kaapo Kamu	2–3
Saana ja Olli, Unto Rautio	4–5
Mikko Ryhänen	6–7
© Matthias Planitzer	8–9
Pietari Hatanpaa	10–11
Kokoro & Moi	12–13
Marko Ahtisaari	22–23
Johannes Romppanen	48–53
Iittala Group	54
Johannes Romppanen	55–57
Design Museum, Helsinki	58–59
Osma Harvilahti	60
Hugh Miller	62–63
Osma Harvilahti	65–66
Hugh Miller	67–69
Jani Kaila	70
Nathalie Lahdenmäki	73
Tyrone Lou	74
Ittala Group	77
Tyrone Lou	78–81
Postal Museum	82–83
Aleksi Niemelä	84
(Top, Bottom right) Aleksi Niemelä	87
(Bottom left) Olle Borgar	87
Aleksi Niemelä	88–93
Osma Harvilahti	94
(Top left) © Marimekko Corporation	97
(Top right, Bottom) Osma Harvilahti	97
Osma Harvilahti	98–100
Design Museum, Helsinki	102
Tapio Wirkkala Rut Bryk Foundation	105
Haarala Hamilton Photography	106–109
Simo Heikkilä	111
Liisa Valonen	112
Simo Heikkilä	114–117
Osma Harvilahti	120–125
Timo Junttila, Iittala Group (Top left, right, Bottom left)	126
Timo Junttila, Iittala Group	127
(Bottom right) Harri Koskinen	127
Osma Harvilahti	128–138
Hugh Miller	139
Osma Harvilahti	140
(Top right) Paramdeep Bahia	141
Osma Harvilahti	141–151
Mikko Ryhänen, © Marimekko Corporation	152–153
Kaapo Kamu	154–155
© Marimekko Corporation	156–165
Johannes Romppanen	166–173
Osma Harvilahti	174–184
(Top) Osma Harvilahti	186
(Bottom) Paramdeep Bahia	186
Osma Harvilahti	187–190
(Left) Design Museum, Helsinki	191
(Right) Osma Harvilahti	191
Design Museum, Helsinki	192–193
Mikko Ryhänen	194
Artek Archive Images	196–201
Johannes Romppanen	202–203
Michael Stavaridis	204–205
Johannes Romppanen	206
Artek Archive Images	207–208
Johannes Romppanen	209–210
Artek Archive Images	211–212
Johannes Romppanen	213
Artek Archive Images	214–215
Marcus Ginns	216
Samuel Bradley	218–220
Marcus Ginns	221–223
(Top) Samuel Bradley	224
(Bottom) Marcus Ginns	224
Samuel Bradley	225–229
(Bottom) Marcus Ginns	229
STK Films	230
Samuel Bradley	231
Paramdeep Bahia	232
Marcus Ginns	234–236
(Top) STK Films	237
(Bottom) Marcus Ginns	237
Marcus Ginns	238–239
Studio Build	240
Marcus Ginns	242–243
Johannes Romppanen	250–255
Aalto Wood Program	256–257
Pekka Heikkinen	258–259
Juho Ajanki	260–265
Johannes Romppanen	266–271
Inga Knölke	272–273
Estelle Hanania	274–279
Paavo Lehtonen	280–285
Kirmo Kivelä	286–291
Ville Lenkkeri	292
Arsi Ikäheimonen, Kekkilä Oy	295
Kuvatoimisto Kuvio Oy	297–299
Verstas Architects	300–303
Iittala Group	306–309
Design Museum, Helsinki	310
Iittala Group	311
Design Museum, Helsinki	312–315
Tapio Wirkkala Rut Bryk Foundation	316–318
(Top, Bottom right) Tapio Wirkkala Rut Bryk Foundation	319
(Bottom left) Iittala Group	319
Tapio Wirkkala Rut Bryk Foundation	320–321
Martti Kapanen, Alvar Aalto Museum	322
(Top) Alvar Aalto Museum	325
(Bottom) Maija Vatanen, Alvar Aalto Museum	325
Hans Jan Dürr	326–327
Alvar Aalto Museum	328
(Top) Alvar Aalto Museum	329
(Bottom) Gustaf Welin, Alvar Aalto Museum	329
Mary Gaudin	330–331
Maija Holma, Alvar Aalto Museum	332
(Top) Gustaf Welin, Alvar Aalto Museum	333
(Bottom) Eva and Pertti Ingervo, Alvar Aalto Museum	333
Artek Archive images	334–339
Iittala Group	340
Johannes Romppanen	343–345
Iittala Group	346–353
Sanna Anukka, Big Active	356–358
© Marimekko Corporation	359
Sanna Anukka, Big Active	360–363
Annika Heikkinen	364
Angel Gil	366
(Top) Angel Gil	367
(Bottom) Liisa Valonen	367
Kaamos Group	368–369
(Top left, Bottom) IMU Design	371
(Top right) © Aava Koti	371
© FontanaArte	372
(Top) Muuto	373
(Bottom) Mika Tolvanen	373
Chikako Harada	374–375
Filippo Podestà	376–377
Chikako Hirada, Aalto University Foundation	378–381
Pro Puu ry	382–383
Samuji	384–391
Ivana Helsinki	392–397
Robin Falck	404–405
Saana ja Olli, Unto Rautio	406–407
Pietari Hatanpaa	408–409
Markus Henttonen	410–411
Maija Savolainen	412–413
Angel Gil	414–415

INDEX

AALTO UNIVERSITY
www.aalto.fi

AAVA KOTI
www.aavakoti.fi

ALVAR AALTO MUSEUM
www.alvaraalto.fi

ANTTO MELASNIEMI
www.anttomelasniemi.fi

ARABIA
www.arabia.fi

ARTEK
www.artek.fi

AVANTO
www.avan.to

AVARTE
www.avarte-cn.com

DENIZEN WORKS
www.denizenworks.com

DESIGN MUSEUM
www.designmuseum.fi

EERO AARNIO
www.eero-aarnio.com

FISKARS
www.fiskars.com

FONTANA ARTE
www.fontanaarte.com

FRIENDS OF FINNISH HANDICRAFTS
www.kasityonystavat.fi

HARRI KOSKINEN
www.harrikoskinen.com
www.friendsofindustry.com

ILMARI TAPIOVAARA
www.ilmaritapiovaara.fi

IITTALA
www.iittala.com

IMU DESIGN
www.imudesign.org

IVANA HELSINKI
www.ivanahelsinki.com

KAAMOS GROUP
www.kaamosgroup.fi

KEKKILÄ GARDEN
www.kekkila.com

KLAUS HAAPANIEMI
www.klaush.com

KULTTUURISAUNA
www.kulttuurisauna.fi

MARIMEKKO
www.marimekko.com

MARI ISOPAHKALA
www.mariisopahkala.fi

MARTI GUIXÉ
www.guixe.com

MUUTO
www.muuto.com

NATHALIE LAHDENMAKI
www.nathalielahdenmaki.fi

NIKARI
www.nikari.fi

NOKIA
www.nokia.com

POSTAL MUSEUM
www.postimuseo.fi

REHTI
www.rehti.org

RUT BRYK
www.wirkkalabryk.fi

SAMUJI
www.samuji.com

SANNA ANNUKKA
www.sanna-annukka.com

SIMO HEIKKILÄ
www.periferiadesign.fi

TAPIO ANTTILA
www.tapioanttila.com

TAPIO WIRKKALA
www.wirkkala.fi

TURNTABLE / DODO
www.kaantopoyta.fi

VERSTAS ARCHITECTS
www.verstasarkkitehdit.fi

VUOKKO NURMESNIEMI
www.vuokko.fi

WIRKKALA BRYK FOUNDATION
www.wirkkalabryk.fi

WOODISM
www.woodism.fi

WOODNOTES
www.woodnotes.fi

YRJÖ KUKKAPURO
www.kukkapuro.fi

CONTRIBUTING PHOTOGRAPHERS

ANGEL GIL
www.angelgil.co.uk

ESTELLE HANANIA
www.estellehanania.com

HAARALA HAMILTON PHOTOGRAPHY
www.haaralahamilton.com

HANS JAN DÜRR
www.durr-architect.nl

INGA KNÖLKE
www.imagekontainer.com

JANI KAILA
www.janikaila.com

JOHANNES ROMPPANEN
www.johannesromppanen.com

JUHO AJANKI
www.juhoajanki.com

KAAPO KAMU
www.kaapokamu.com

LIISA VALONEN
www.liisavalonen.com

MAIJA SAVOLAINEN
www.maijasavolainen.com

MARCUS GINNS
www.marcusginnsphotography.co.uk

MARKUS HENTTONEN
www.markushenttonen.com

MARY GAUDIN
www.marygaudin.com

MICHAEL STAVARIDIS
www.stavphoto.com

MIKKO RYHÄNEN
www.mikkoryhanen.org

OSMA HARVILAHTI
www.osma.fi

PAAVO LEHTONEN
www.paavolehtonen.com

PIETARI HATANPAA
www.pietarihatanpaa.com

SAMUEL BRADLEY
www.samuelbradley.com

UNTO RAUTIO
www.untorautio.com

VILLE LENKKERI
www.villelenkkeri.com

CONTRIBUTING WRITERS

FIONA THOMPSON
www.wordspring.co.uk

IDA KUKKAPURO
www.idakukkapuro.com

JIM DAVIES
www.totalcontent.co.uk

LAURA IISALO
www.lauraiisalo.com

THANKS TO

Jarkko Airamaa
Taavetti Alin
Margaretha Andreassen
Hanna Anonen
Pirkko Attila
Jesper Bange
Linda Bergroth
Kam Bhogal
Giorgio Biscaro
Alison Bracegirdle
Sue Breakell
Greg Burne
Laura Cavanagh
Alastair Coe
Charlotte Crouch
Tom Dixon
Suvi-Elina Enqvist
Ulla Eronen
Anton Fahlberg
Filipa Forder
Matthew George
Taina Grönqvist
Sonia Guareschi
Heli Haapkylä
Maria Härkäpää
Lauri Harvilhati
Maarit Heikkilä
Annika Heikkinen
Pekka Heikkinen
Salla Heino
Marjo Holma
Emma Houldren
Mikko Hyvärinen
Arsi Ikäheimonen
Anu Iso-Kokkila-Vähänen
Päivi Jantunen
Janne Joukas
Jani Kaila
Sanna-Kaisa Niikko
Minna Kajava
Antti J. Kallio
Silja Kaurala
Smriti Khanna
Krista Kinnunen
Kristiina Kobayashi
Marketa Kolíbal
Stanislav Kolíbal
Saara Koskinen
Irmeli Kukkapuro
Wataru Kumano
Sirpa Kutilainen
Simon Lamason
Hanna-Leena Markus
Tyrone Lou

Johanna Luhtala
Mark Mason
Liisa Mayow
Jenni Mikkonen
Hannu Mikola
Asta Mikonsaari
Catherine Moriarty
Jasper Morrison
Jodi Mullen
Greta Muuri
Karan Nigam
Siru Nori
Chihiro Ohama
Sari Ojaniemi-Mäkelä
Eamonn O'Reilly
Helena Pärssinen
Minna Pasanen
Filippo Podestà
Anders Portman
Jukka Puljujärvi
Heli Puputti
Risto Raittila
Janne Rät
Jopsu Ramu
Timo Ramu
Tuomas Reivo
Mikko Ryhänen
Karola Sahi
Arttu Salovaara
Laura Sarvilinna
Jukka Savolainen
Rick Sellars
Kirsikka Simberg
Leena Sipponen
Martin Sommerschield
Paola Suhonen
Pirjo Suhonen
Aila Svenskberg
Laura Syrjala
Sawa Tanaka
Anne Tapanainen
Jaana Taskinen
Philip Tidwell
Veronika Träger
Mika Tolvanen
Elina Turpeinen
Markus Tuomivaara
Marttiina Utriainen
Liisa Valonen
Marta Valtonen
Johanna Vuorio
Mia Wallenius
Hetty Wessels